Elite • 182

Prussian Napoleonic Tactics 1792–1815

PETER HOFSCHRÖER

ILLUSTRATED BY ADAM HOOK

Series editor Martin Windrow

First published in Great Britain in 2011 by Osprey Publishing,
Midland House, West Way, Botley, Oxford, OX2 0PH, UK
44-02 23rd Street, Suite 219, Long Island City, NY 11101, USA
E-mail: info@ospreypublishing.com

Osprey Publishing is part of the Osprey Group

A CIP catalogue record for this book is available from the British Library

Print ISBN: 978 1 84603 509 8
PDF ebook ISBN: 978 1 84908 300 3
ePub ebook ISBN: 978 1 84908 882 4

Editor: Martin Windrow
Page layout by: Ken Vail Graphic Design, Cambridge, UK (kvgd.com)
Index by Auriol Griffith-Jones
Typeset in Sabon and Myriad Pro
Originated by PDQ Digital Media Solutions, Suffolk, UK
Printed in China through Worldprint Ltd

11 12 13 14 15 10 9 8 7 6 5 4 3 2 1

Osprey Publishing is supporting the Woodland Trust, the UK's leading
woodland conservation charity, by funding the dedication of trees.

www.ospreypublishing.com

ARTIST'S NOTE

Readers may care to note that the original paintings from which the colour
plates in this book were prepared are available for private sale. All
reproduction copyright whatsoever is retained by the Publishers. All
enquiries should be addressed to:

Scorpio Gallery, PO Box 475, Hailsham, E. Sussex BN27 2SL, UK

The Publishers regret that they can enter into no correspondence upon this
matter.

ACKNOWLEDGEMENT

The author wishes to record his gratitude to Oliver Schmidt for his help in
securing certain illustrations used in this book.

CONTENTS

PRUSSIAN NAPOLEONIC TACTICS 1792–1815

THE LEGACY OF FREDERICK THE GREAT

'The [Prussian] army itself was largely a parade-ground façade, composed in large part of mercenaries, both officers and men' – thus Elting, in his *Military History and Atlas of the Napoleonic Wars* (1964).

'In doctrine, however, the Prussian army was hopelessly outdated in its concepts. Everything was related to the days of Frederick the Great, and deviations from the Master's precepts were not countenanced' – thus Chandler, in his *The Campaigns of Napoleon* (1988).

'Tactically, the Prussian Army was a museum piece' – thus Fuller, in his *Decisive Battles of the Western World* (1970).

'It is clear then that the old and the new were already struggling with one another in Prussia before 1806, but in every important respect the old was unshaken, and the army, in its composition, was still completely of the old Frederican type' – thus Delbrück, in his *Dawn of Modern Warfare* (1990).

The bulk of the Prussian army consisted of 'demoralized men, often the dregs of society, press-ganged foreigners and prisoners of war, unwilling peasants and unreliable mercenaries, the whole motley crew held together by violent brutal discipline and ferocious punishments' – thus Kitchen, in his *Military History of Germany* (1975).

'When, in 1806, the precise linear tactics of Frederick came into contact with the more mobile system of the French, they failed absolutely… The Prussian attacks on Vierzehnheiligen were a good example of the impossibility of succeeding with the parade ground tactics of the Seven Years' War against the new tactics of the French' – thus Petre, in his *Napoleon's Conquest of Prussia* (1977). In his *Jena Campaign* (1909), Maude describes the same action, when there 'followed one of the most extraordinary and pitiful incidents in military history. The line of magnificent Infantry, some 20,000 strong, stood out in the open for two whole hours whilst exposed to the merciless case and skirmishing fire of the French, who behind their garden walls offered no mark at all for their return fire.'

'That army marched away to Jena and Auerstadt [sic], tried gallantly to fight its battle in Frederick's style: stiff lines of musketeers trampling slowly forward or standing in the open while Lannes' scarce-seen skirmishers used

Frederick the Great at the end of his life. Some claim that for years after his death his conservative influence prevented the modernization of the Prussian army. However, the record shows that both during his latter years and after his death reforms were steadily introduced. (Richard Knötel; author's collection)

them for target practice; yelling, disorderly squadrons crowding in through the morning fog to splinter against Davout's squares. The rest was an increasingly despairing retreat, and disaster piled upon defeat' – thus Elting once more, in his *Swords Around the Throne* (1997).

'Ordered to deploy within musket range of the latter [the French], the former [Prussian infantry] dutifully went through the intricate manoeuvres of the Frederickian drill while being riddled with sniper fire… Seeking neither to retire nor to advance, they stood stoically before the French positions for perhaps 90 minutes' – thus Gates, in his *The British Light Infantry Arm* (1987).

These damning verdicts are the received wisdom. However, there is a counter-argument for a much more careful analysis of the sources.

In his book *Preussen ohne Legend*, Sebastian Haffner comments: 'For believers in this myth, which even today is stuck fast in many heads, the twenty years of Prussian history from 1795 to 1815 fall into two sharply contrasting periods, as black and white as the Prussian flag. The years of the Peace of Basle with Revolutionary France were, according to this view, a period of stagnation and decadence for which the collapse of 1806 was payment; and the period from 1808 to 1812 was a time of courageous reform, regeneration, and preparation for the uprising that one could say occurred according to programme, and was rewarded with the victorious Wars of Liberation.

We must get away from this myth. It is not only an oversimplification; it is a falsification of history. This period is in reality one unit. The same people and forces were at work the whole time…'.

Which, if either, of these diametrically opposed views is correct? To establish that, we must look at the development of the Prussian army from the end of the Seven Years' War up to the battle of Jena, and beyond.

THE LATE FREDERICKIAN ARMY

At the end of the Seven Years' War in 1763, Frederick the Great's army, which had at one time taken on and defeated the armies of the major powers of Continental Europe, had an unenviable reputation. It had been the most modern of its day, the model that other armies emulated, but after such a long, exhausting war there was little of it left to emulate. The pool of native conscripts had been depleted, to be filled out with deserters and prisoners from opposing armies. Frederick described them as being no more capable than an inexperienced militia, so his first post-war reform was to restore the quality of the army.

At this time, Brandenburg-Prussia's economy was basically agrarian, with agricultural production generating the larger part of the national revenues. The so-called 'Inländer', or native conscripts, provided the backbone of the army; the bulk of them were farm boys, who underwent a period of basic training before being assigned to the reserve. Once in the reserve, they would be called up for refresher courses during the autumn manoeuvres. Being of greater economic value, the professional classes, skilled artisans and tradesmen were exempted from military service. The landowning classes, the 'Junkers', provided the officer corps; they were born and brought up on the same estates as the soldiers they commanded, and the army and civil population were inextricably linked. Contrary to popular myth, the army was at this time very much part of society, providing several public services in the garrison towns, including education, healthcare and policing. Part of its manpower was also provided by volunteers, professional soldiers; these are often referred to as 'foreign mercenaries', but this is an incorrect translation of the term 'Ausländer', a word with a number of meanings in German (see below, 'Inländer and Ausländer').

WEAPONS AND THEIR EMPLOYMENT

The basic battle-drills of the Frederickian army were typical of all contemporary armies, being based on making the most effective use of the arms technology of the period. The standard armament of the line infantry was a muzzle-loading smoothbore musket, approximately accurate to no more than 50 to 75 paces, and the only effective way of employing these was to concentrate as many of them as possible, and fire simultaneous disciplined volleys. The object was to point whole battalions, not individual weapons (it would be wrong to use the term 'aim' in the context of smoothbore weapons used en masse). The 'line' infantry earned this name from their tactical use; battles consisted, in great part, of lines of infantry pouring as many volleys as possible into the enemy line until one or the other gave way. Given the complex process for loading and firing a muzzle-loading musket, the battle-drills required to achieve this result demanded a considerable amount of time-consuming, repetitive training.

Although the optimal method of delivering fire was to pack as many men as possible into the firing line, attempts to use four ranks – two standing, two kneeling in front of them – proved too demanding. This gave way to the use of just three ranks – two standing, one kneeling. As the 18th century progressed, the duration and quality of training were diluted by the growth in the size of armies, and it increasingly became the norm for just the first two ranks to deliver volleys, with the third evolving into a reserve that began to be used for special purposes. When firing volleys, it was important to achieve a level of training high enough to avoid the firers inflicting injuries on their comrades. The second rank had to lock into the gaps in the front rank in such a way that neither their muzzle-flash nor the considerable flash of their priming pans injured the men in the front rank. This required the instilling of a culture of exact obedience to orders for sequences of strictly disciplined movements. Failure to follow the battle-drills closely would result in a reduction in the effectiveness of the battalion.

In his later years, after the Seven Years' War, Frederick devoted attention to improving the design of the infantry musket to deliver more rapid fire. The 1782 pattern Prussian musket was no less accurate than the British 'Brown Bess', though less so than the French Charleville, and it did have several design advantages over these contemporaries. These included a 'cylindrical'

Fusiliers of the Prussian Guard, 1813; they are deployed in a skirmish line in pairs, with one man covering the other while he loads, and an officer directing the fire. Contrary to popular myth, Frederick's early contempt for Austria's Croat irregulars did not blind him to his army's need for a properly constituted body of trained light infantry. Before his death three 'free regiments' were raised in addition to the regular rifle-armed Jäger regiment, and the first formal Instruction for the employment of these troops was issued. The raising in 1787–88 of fusilier battalions, with a special weapon and a manual of tactical drills, also preceded by some years the Revolutionary Wars – despite some claims that the French Revolutionary armies introduced the first effective large-scale skirmishing tactics for regular troops. (Thümen; author's collection)

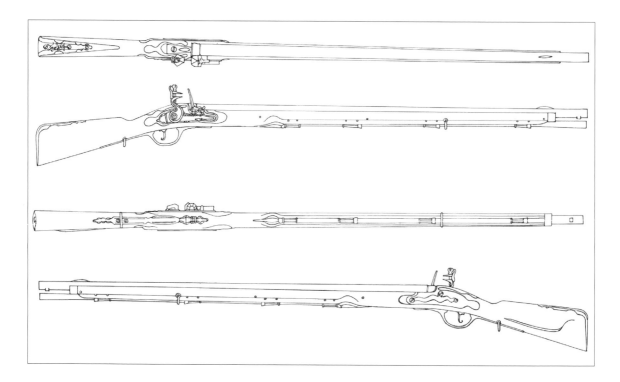

Prussian infantry musket of the 1740/89 patterns. During dispersed manufacture throughout that timespan it went through repeated minor modifications, but the basic model in use in the Revolutionary and Napoleonic period is usually termed the 1782 pattern. It seems inexplicable that Clausewitz called the 1782 the 'worst musket in Europe'. In comparative trials ordered by Gen Scharnhorst in 1813, firing 200 shots at a target representing an enemy line 6ft high and 100ft wide, the 1782 achieved 46 per cent hits at 100 paces – very similar to the results achieved with the British 'Brown Bess'. Both were markedly inferior to the French M1777/1802 Charleville, which achieved 75 per cent hits; however, a modified 1782 pattern with an improved butt shape, which saw some use in 1813–14, achieved similar results to the Charleville. (By kind permission of Biblio-Verlag, Osnabrück)

ramrod rather than one with a swollen end; thus it did not need to be turned around after being withdrawn from its pipes in order to ram home the charge. The barrel had a bias-cut base-plug combined with a touchhole of slightly conical section – i.e. narrowing from the inside of the barrel to the outside where it met the priming pan. This allowed the closed pan to be primed automatically from the inside of the barrel as the powder charge was rammed home, instead of having to be primed from the outside in a separate series of movements. These features reduced the number of evolutions involved in reloading, shaving seconds off the time needed between volleys and giving the Prussians a tactical advantage in a fire-fight. Firing blanks in training, a battalion could let off 30 volleys in seven to eight minutes – well over three shots per minute. Those who describe the use of Prussian battle-drills as a 'slavish adherence to tactical inflexibility' do not appear to fully grasp the practicalities of fighting with 18th-century muskets.

Further reforms in the latter years of Frederick's reign came in the Infantry Regulations of 1771. These included increasing the marching speed to 75 paces per minute, and deploying battalions into line directly from divisional (half-company) columns, as opposed to a column of battalions. Frederick also founded the regular light infantry, the experience of the Seven Years' War having convinced him of the need for such an arm. Frederick's cavalry reached its peak in the Seven Years' War, with the Cavalry Regulations of 1764 being merely a reprint of earlier instructions. Well mounted and well trained, this arm performed just as well in the campaign of 1778 (the War of the Bavarian Succession) as it had done 16 years earlier.

INLÄNDER AND AUSLÄNDER

As mentioned, the Prussian army drew its manpower from two sources. Half the men were to be conscripted from the population of the local 'canton' or catchment area, the other half being volunteers recruited outside this area. Exempting skilled labour and taking the less educated countrymen for military service was a time-honoured way of minimizing the disruption to the local economy. Those exempt from conscription included the wealthy, the professions, business people, industrialists, and the sons of civil servants; skilled artisans, those performing important duties on the landowners' estates, and only sons who were due to inherit a farm; and also the colonists of those marshy areas that were then being reclaimed, since their work was considered to be of national importance.

When they had reached their 20th year, the conscripts were called up for one year, but usually served for only ten months before being sent on furlough or leave. Thereafter they were required to be available for military service as needed, normally until their 40th year. A selected number of these men were called back to their regiments for the two-month-long annual exercises, and in time of war. An army half of which consisted of, in effect, part-time soldiers needed to have a reliable full-time element if it was to function properly. That was the role of the recruits known as Ausländer, who signed up for a longer period.

These men were drawn from outside the regiment's local area. One of the meanings of Ausländer is indeed 'foreigner', but that is not its only meaning. The root-word *Land* can mean nation, state, province, land, country and countryside. An Ausländer in the context of the Prussian army of this time was not necessarily a non-German, or even a non-Prussian, but simply a soldier recruited either from outside the canton or from among those normally exempt from military service. For instance, in 1788, Blücher's squadron of hussars contained 79 such recruits, of which only ten were non-Germans: five Poles, two Hungarians, one Bohemian, one Swede and one Italian. Of the remainder, 18 came from Prussia's core provinces, 19 from the newly-acquired West Prussia, three were soldiers' sons, 11 were Saxons, six Mecklenburgers, three from Anhalt, three from Danzig, two from Ansbach-Bayreuth, and one each from Hesse, Brunswick, Swabia and Alsace. These proportions were not atypical for the Prussian army in this period.

The use of the term 'mercenary' to describe such men is emotive to modern ears, since it gives an impression of unscrupulous freebooters going around offering their services to the highest bidder. They were in fact men of diverse backgrounds, who signed up for a given period in return for pay and provisions – much like any professional soldier today. Then, as throughout history, joining the army was a good way for a young man to escape the constraints of home, get a half-decent set of clothes and ensure regular meals.

For many, their regiment became their home for years, if not for life. For instance, the full-timers in Blücher's squadron were aged between 19 and 52 years old; half were between 27 and 41, a quarter were younger than that, and a quarter older. Thirty-five of these men had served for between ten and 20 years, 14 for over 20 years, and one for 29 years; on average, these men had given 13 years of service each. Far from being 'unreliable mercenaries', they were much better soldiers than the part-time local conscripts. Blücher once commented that his full-timers were 'good men – something can be done with them', while describing his conscripts as 'dumb'. (It is interesting that the full-timers' nickname for a part-time conscript called up for refresher training and the annual field exercises was *Speckmichel* or 'fatty'.) The careless impression of the human composition of the Prussian army created by some historians thus bears little resemblance to reality.

The basic infantry instruction manuals in use during the Napoleonic period remained, with only minor up-dating, the basis for battle-drills for many years after 1815. Although the men wear post-Napoleonic uniform, these illustrations show drill postures unchanged since at least the 1812 Regulations.

LEFT
A three-man file of infantry about to give fire; the third rank took a step backwards, while the front two presented and fired.

MIDDLE
Three figures showing variations in the 'shouldering arms' posture. From left to right: an NCO carrying his musket with fixed bayonet at his right side; a Guard private, shouldering his weapon on the left; and a Jäger, carrying his shorter rifle at the right side, without the bayonet.

RIGHT
Privates 'trailing arms', and 'charging arms'. (Lieder/Jügel; author's collection)

THE EARLY REFORMS, 1783–92

The experience of the Seven Years' War, and particularly the lessons taught by the Croatian border troops employed by the Austrians, led Frederick the Great to consider founding an effective counterforce. Events during the War of the Bavarian Succession (1778–79) underlined this need, and three 'Free Regiments' were raised to complement the regiment of riflemen or *Fussjäger* already in existence. An 'Instruction for the Free Regiments' was published in 1783, two years before Frederick's death. His nephew Frederick William II, who ascended to the throne in 1785, continued to reform and modernize the army. His predecessor's general staff had been simply an advisory body appointed for the campaign in question; one of Frederick William II's reforms was to make the staff a permanent body, with a set structure.[1]

The organization of the infantry was radically altered. Only the four battalions of Guards kept their structure of five musketeer companies and a flank grenadier company. An order-in-cabinet of 27 February 1787 abolished the previous distinction between types of infantry regiment; from 1 June that year, each regiment was to consist of one battalion of grenadiers and two of musketeers. Each battalion now had its own commander (a major), so the regimental colonel, who was likely to be a brigade or divisional general, no longer commanded one of the battalions in person. Discounting supernumeraries, a battalion had four companies, each of about 152 enlisted men subdivided into two divisions (*Züge*), each of two platoons (*Peletone*). The company formed up in 44 three-man files, giving the battalion in line about 176 files. (The formation of a battalion line is illustrated in Plate A.)

The 'book' strength of a regiment included 55 officers, consisting of the colonel, a lieutenant-colonel, 4 majors (including one supernumerary), 6 captains, 5 (from 1790, 6) junior captains, 3 aides-de-camp (battalion adjutants), and 35 (from 1790, 34) subalterns. The regimental establishment included 144 NCOs, consisting of 12 sergeant-majors, 36 sergeants, 36 senior corporals, and 60 corporals; in addition, 3 artillery NCOs commanded the pairs of battalion guns, with 51 gunners drawn from the ranks. There were 39 drummers (including one regimental and two battalion drummers).

1 For further details, see my Men-at-Arms 381: *Prussian Staff & Specialist Troops 1791–1815*.

The rest of the rank-and-file were 240 junior corporals and 1,320 privates, plus 120 supernumeraries.

Also in 1787, ten 'Schützen' (marksmen, sharpshooters) were added to each company of line infantry; armed with rifled carbines, these men provided a skirmishing element. They were deployed to the rear of the line with the NCOs, and wore NCOs' uniform distinctions. From May 1793 each regiment, and from that December each battalion, replaced one drummer with a bugler (hornist), who relayed commands to the Schützen section. In that same year, the first fusilier (light infantry) battalions were formed (see below, 'Light troops').

The Regulations issued on 13 September 1788 remained in force, with various amendments, until 1806 and indeed beyond. Pre-dating the French Revolution, this was one of the most modern drill manuals of its day. There had been no changes in weaponry, so the 1788 manual essentially made no alterations to battle-drills, but there were some simplifications in the handling of the firearms, with a number of the evolutions being confined to the paradeground only. Furthermore, less emphasis was placed on the rate of fire and more on pointing the weapons. Volley fire was the preferred way of engaging enemy infantry, with fire by half-company divisions being used against cavalry, as this always left a number of men with muskets loaded and ready to counter any sudden move by enemy horsemen.

The King's Regiment (No.18), 1805, showing how Prussian infantry presented arms throughout the period. The officer, holding a broad-bladed spontoon, stands in front of his men; behind him a drummer waits to pass his orders, and in the left background a senior NCO is identified by his long half-pike. (Thümen; author's collection)

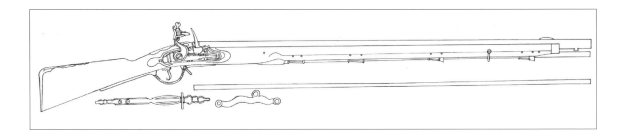

LIGHT TROOPS

The section of the 1788 Regulations covering the use of the Schützen was entirely new, and this was published separately on 26 February 1789 as an Instruction. The Schützen spent two weeks each year on target practice, normally under the instruction of a specially selected officer. One of the infantry company's 12 senior NCOs was designated the Schützen NCO, and was also armed with a rifled carbine. These marksmen were trained to fight in the same fashion as the Fussjäger or Rifle Regiment, in woods, undergrowth, cropland, and in broken country among ditches or rocks. They were also intended to be used for outposts and patrols, securing the line of march. On the field of battle they were to be deployed 100 paces in front of their battalion to harass the enemy and cover the unit while it moved into effective range; once the battalion was engaged, the Schützen were to fall back to its flanks. However, the emphasis remained on the use of volley fire and the bayonet attack by infantry in three-deep lines, so the role of these infantry company marksmen on the battlefield was merely to cover the line's movement until it was close enough to engage the enemy.[2]

First formed in 1787, the fusilier battalions received their own drill manual on 24 February 1788. They formed up in two ranks, not the customary three of the line regiments, which facilitated their deployment into individual pairs of skirmishers. They were dressed in green, as was traditional for huntsmen; they were armed with a lighter 1787-pattern fusilier musket, and did not carry colours. Each battalion had four companies, and totalled 19 officers, 48 sergeants, 13 musicians (each company had two buglers and a drummer, and there was one battalion bugler), 80 corporals and 440 privates, plus 40 supernumeraries. As in the line units, each company had ten rifle-armed Schützen. On mobilization, each battalion received a 3-pdr gun served by artillerymen. The wartime strength of a fusilier battalion was 680 combatants and 56 non-combatants, with each of the four companies theoretically having 90 Inländer conscripts and 75 Ausländer recruits.

Confusingly, the terms for fusilier sub-units were the reverse of those used in musketeer units: each fusilier company consisted of two 'platoons', each of two 'divisions'. When conducting skirmish attacks, the 1st and 8th Platoons were deployed (i.e. one-quarter of the battalion); the 5th and 7th Platoons could be used to support or replace them, while the other half of the battalion formed a reserve in line. Bugle-horn signals were used to give orders for advancing, deploying into skirmish order, loading, opening and ceasing fire, moving to the left or right, withdrawing and rallying. Even when in close order, horn signals were given for opening and ceasing fire, particularly when 'firing at will'. Emphasis was placed on field training

2 For further details, see my Men-at-Arms 149, *Prussian Light Infantry 1792–1815*.

and combat leadership. As the Prussian officer corps still contained many experienced former officers of 'free corps' and veterans of the war in North America, such as Gneisenau and Schuler von Senden, the fusilier battalions soon enjoyed an élite reputation.

The evolution of the infantryman towards a soldier capable of flexible employment continued as the 18th century drew to a close. For instance, before the start of the Revolutionary Wars, Duke Carl William Ferdinand of Brunswick-Lüneburg (a Prussian senior commander) published an Instruction on the use of the under-employed third-rank men of line battalions as skirmishers, and the detachment from the line of separate platoons for special use, such as skirmishing on the battlefield and providing flank guards on the march.

CAVALRY

An Instruction of 6 March 1787 set the strengths of the categories of cavalry regiment as follows:

Cuirassiers – 37 officers, 80 NCOs, 11 trumpeters, 660 troopers,
    60 supernumeraries
Dragoons – 37 officers, 75 NCOs, 16 trumpeters, 660 troopers,
    60 supernumeraries
Hussars – 51 officers, 150 NCOs, 30 trumpeters, 1,320 troopers
Garde du Corps (Life Guards) – Three squadrons strong, with 24 officers,
    48 NCOs, 8 musicians and 522 troopers.

Each squadron of cuirassiers included ten men armed with rifled carbines, while each dragoon and hussar squadron had 12 carabineers. These men practised target firing, and were considered potential NCO material. In 1787 the dragoons gave up their bayonets, and in 1790 the cuirassiers gave up their cuirasses. Attention was paid to encouraging the use of horses bred at home rather than using imports. The cuirassiers rode black and brown horses, while most hussar regiments favoured the more nimble East European breeds. Plans to introduce a new set of regulations for the cavalry in February 1792 were interrupted by the outbreak of the Revolutionary Wars, and delayed until 1796.

ARTILLERY

The artillery was reorganized in 1787 into four regiments of equal strength, each of 54 officers, 360 NCOs, 1,600 gunners, 10 surgeons, 8 oboists and 10 or 11 drummers.

From 1787, the ordnance was modernized and upgraded. The light 12-pdrs were withdrawn from service, melted down and recast as heavy 6-pounders. Howitzers were no longer used as battalion guns, but distributed among the field batteries. The number of pieces in a battery was reduced from ten to eight, including two howitzers. A total of 66 batteries were available, including:

6 bombardment batteries, each of 6x heavy 12-pdrs and 2x heavy
    10lb howitzers
22 medium 12-pdr batteries, each of 6x medium 12-pdrs and 2x light
    10lb howitzers

16 heavy 6-pdr batteries, each of 6x heavy 6-pdr and 2x light 10lb howitzers
16 light 6-pdr batteries, each of 6x light 6-pdrs and 2x 7lb howitzers
6 horse artillery brigades, each of 8x light 6-pdrs and one 7lb howitzer

The field army had a total of 920 artillery pieces available, including 188x 6-pdrs and 132x 3-pdrs dispersed as battalion guns with the infantry, 20x light 3-pdrs with the fusiliers, and 46 reserve guns. In 1790 the field artillery was augmented by two batteries each of 8x light 10lb mortars.

An order-in-cabinet of 1 October 1791 outlined a reorganization of the artillery into 60 batteries. The field artillery was to consist of ten batteries of medium 12-pdrs, 16 of heavy 6-pdrs, and ten of light 6-pounders. The horse artillery was to have six batteries of light 6-pounders. The reserve artillery was to consist of four bombardment batteries, four batteries of medium 12-pdrs, four of heavy 6-pdrs, four of light 6-pdrs, two of 10lb mortars, and ten 3-pdr guns. The number of battalion guns did not change. The total of 836 pieces consisted of 162x 3-pdrs, 320x light and 120x heavy 6-pdrs, 84 medium 12-pdrs, 24x bombardment pieces, 34x 7lb and 76x 10lb howitzers, plus 16x mortars.

A **MUSKETEER BATTALION IN LINE, c. 1792**

This plate shows an infantry battalion in three ranks. Ideally, the men should have been able to fire in three ranks, with the front rank kneeling. However, the dilution in the quality of trained manpower that accompanied the expansion of European armies towards the end of the 18th century made it more practical to have just the front two ranks firing from a standing position, the second rank firing through the intervals in the first, while the third rank took a pace to the rear.

A Prussian infantry battalion of the Revolutionary Wars consisted of four companies, each of two divisions; these eight half-company divisions were the basic units of command and manoeuvre. The average company had a captain commander and three subaltern officers, 12 senior NCOs and about 140 junior NCOs and privates, giving about 44–46 three-man files, so that the battalion occupied a frontage of some 250 yards. The company captain **(C)** and his senior lieutenant **(L)** each took post at the right-hand end of the front rank of one division; behind them was an empty space, with an NCO file-closer in the rear rank. At each flank of the battalion the ranks were closed by an officer **(O)** backed by two NCOs **(N)**. The other NCOs were spaced along and about four paces behind the rear of their companies, as were the ten Schützen in each company **(S)**, and the remaining officers stood a pace or two behind them. The battalion's major **(M)** and the adjutant **(A)** remained mounted, taking post behind the outer divisions of the 1st and 4th Companies; the three drummers from each company were assembled in two blocks of six behind these companies **(D)**. Each company also had eight supernumeraries on strength, and these 32 extra men were assembled in a single block behind the centre **(SN)**, under a senior NCO; they were used to plug any gaps in the battle line caused by casualties.

The colour party **(CP)** was positioned in the centre of the battalion, the cadets carrying the two flags (respectively, the Avancierfahne and Retirierfahne) in the front and rear ranks. In a regimental 1st Bn, as here, these differed in design; the former

was the Leibfahne or 'colonel's colour', and the latter one of the three Regimentersfahnen; in a 2nd Bn, both flags were Regimentersfahnen. The colour-bearers were guarded by the four company sergeant-majors, flanked on each side by nine men in three files. The colour party and escort took no part in the volley-firing. In grenadier battalions, prior to the 1787 regulations, six fifers were assembled behind the colour party; we show their position **(F)**, though by 1792 they had been discontinued in any except Guard grenadier battalions. Beside them, an orderly holds the battalion commander's horse; the commanding officer himself **(CO)** took position on foot in front of his battalion.

The role of the unit commander was to point his entire battalion to ensure that their fire was as effective as possible. With the first two ranks of a battalion line totalling some 400 men, each capable of firing at least two rounds per minute and often three, a Prussian battalion in line could deliver in one minute at least the same number of rounds as the practical rate of fire of a modern machine gun.

Inset 1: One of the two battalion guns, placed on the right flank of the line. The crews were provided by infantrymen under the supervision of an artillery NCO and a mounted artillery officer. When armies were stationary the guns were positioned about 50 yards ahead of the intervals in the line. When the advancing line caught up with them they were moved fowards with the infantry by means of bricoles. When the line got within about 400 yards of the enemy the guns halted and opened fire with roundshot, keeping this up until their battalion was engaged with the enemy. They then advanced again, to within about 75 yards' range, and opened fire with case-shot (canister). Battalion guns attached to the units in the second line only opened fire if the first line was defeated and retreated through the second line.

Inset 2: The officer and two senior NCOs posted to close the ranks at each end of the battalion line. Their spontoons/ half-pikes were generally discontinued from 1807 onwards, when NCOs (theoretically) received rifled carbines.

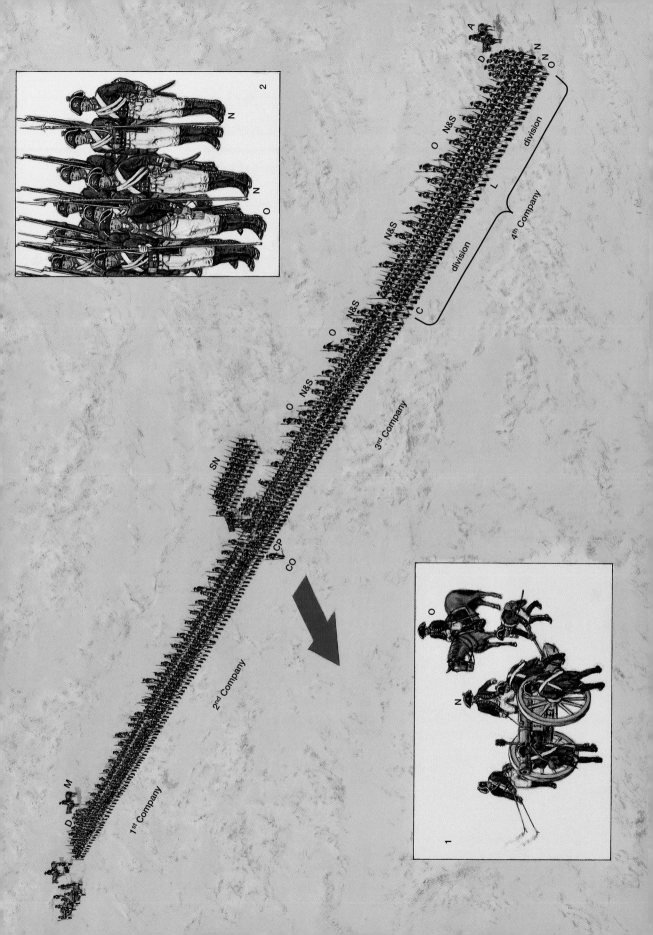

1st Company

2nd Company

3rd Company

4th Company

division

division

D
M

CO
CP

SN

O
N&S

O
N&S

O
N&S

O
N&S

C
L
N
D
A

N
N
O

2

N

N

O

1

O

N

THE EXPERIENCE OF THE REVOLUTIONARY WARS

The Prussian army thus went to war against Revolutionary France in 1792 with a modern set of drill regulations, a well-designed musket, well-trained men, well-mounted troopers, modern artillery and confident officers. This army would hold its own in the coming campaigns. Referring back to the charges quoted at the beginning of this text: once battle commenced, was the Prussian army actually 'inflexible', and did the 'precise linear tactics of Frederick the Great' really make it a 'museum piece' compared with other armies?

VALMY

Much hot air has been expended on the 'cannonade of Valmy' in September 1792, which was the first occasion on which the French Revolutionary army did not run at the mere sight of the enemy. It certainly marked an important turning point, but from a tactical viewpoint it was of little significance.

The Prussian vanguard under the Prince of Hohenlohe deployed in an exemplary fashion – according to Lt Knesebeck of Duke Karl August's Regiment, in such an orderly manner that it might have been a single regiment. It consisted of 11 battalions of foot, 30 squadrons of horse and 5½ batteries of artillery.

Three battalions of fusiliers drew up in front of the main body of line infantry, while five companies of Jägers formed a skirmish line ahead of them

Sharpshooter's carbine, 1787. This specially designed rifled weapon, produced for the Schützen section of the line infantry companies, was yet another Prussian innovation. (By kind permission of Biblio-Verlag, Osnabrück)

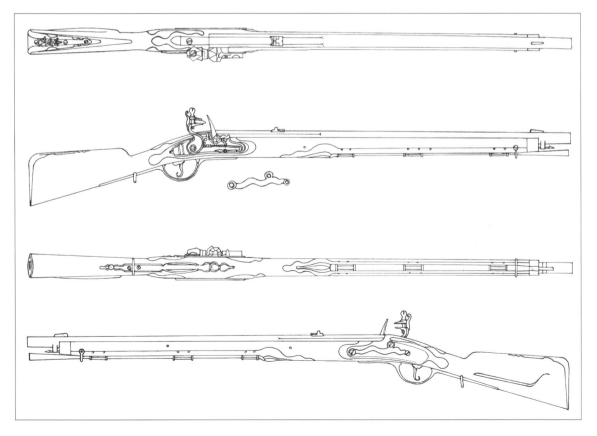

(a deployment reminiscent of those prescribed in the supposedly innovative 1812 Regulations). The Prussian vanguard covered the deployment of the main body of the army under Duke Karl August of Saxe-Weimar. Due to the damp weather the men had not loaded their muskets, but they now did so, shouldering their arms and marching towards Dumouriez's army for 100 to 200 paces. The infantry then halted while the artillery was brought up; the guns unlimbered and fired on the French for several hours, finishing at 5 p.m. Early on, the windmill at Valmy was set alight and the flames spread to a number of French ammunition wagons, which then exploded, causing a panic. Nevertheless order was soon restored, and the French stood their ground. The Duke of Brunswick, commanding the Prussian army here, decided not to take the risk of attacking the French. Losses that day amounted to only a couple of hundred men on each side. From a tactical perspective, there is little to say about Valmy. The Prussian infantry deployed according to its battle-drills, but was not engaged in combat.

After Valmy, however, the French went onto the offensive, and the war moved from France into the Netherlands and the Rhineland in 1793–94. After the French garrison in Mainz capitulated to the Allied forces on 4 July 1793, the latter then moved westwards again, and as they did so there were a number of clashes. When the Prussian forces were fighting in the Palatinate and on the Lower Rhine in western Germany, the expertise of their light troops in particular – fusiliers, Jägers and hussars – brought success in many combats, before the weight of French numbers finally took its toll.

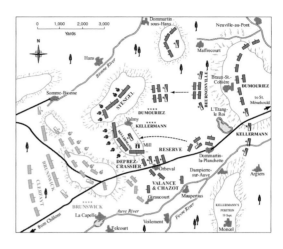

Battle of Valmy, 20 September 1792. The Duke of Brunswick's Prussian army (pale blocks, low left) faced Dumouriez's and Kellerman's French army, which was drawn up around the famous windmill. The infantry of both sides deployed in line, but did not engage in a fire-fight. The tactical battle-drills of the two armies hardly differed. (*The Encyclopedia of the French Revolutionary and Napoleonic Wars*, ed. G. Fremont-Barnes; p.1034)

FRISANGE

At dawn on 12 September 1793 the then-Colonel von Blücher, commanding the 8th Hussar Regiment, rode out to investigate the sound of firing. After riding for an hour and a half he saw a line of French infantry drawn up with its right flank against the village of Frisange, so he sent his aide Lt Count Goltz to bring up three squadrons of his regiment. The first two were ordered to join Blücher, while the third was to swing round to the right, through woods, and then meet up with him. All were to keep under cover as much as possible. Blücher described what happened next in his Journal: 'As the enemy appeared to want to withdraw, I rode with my two orderlies into the imperial [Austrian] skirmishers and urged them to engage the enemy, as I feared the French would withdraw before my squadrons could arrive… At last I saw my squadrons coming. The horses were exhausted, which is why I had them form up behind the village to catch their breath'. The surprise was total; Blücher now put himself at the head of his two squadrons, and

> went right through the village. I had one squadron deploy to the right of the highway, the other to the left, next to 20 Zerbst cavalrymen [a contingent from a small German state] who happened to be there, whom I ordered to hold the road. Then I charged the enemy infantry. The enemy cavalry tried to stop us, but we chased them off. The infantry were marching to reach a small wood behind

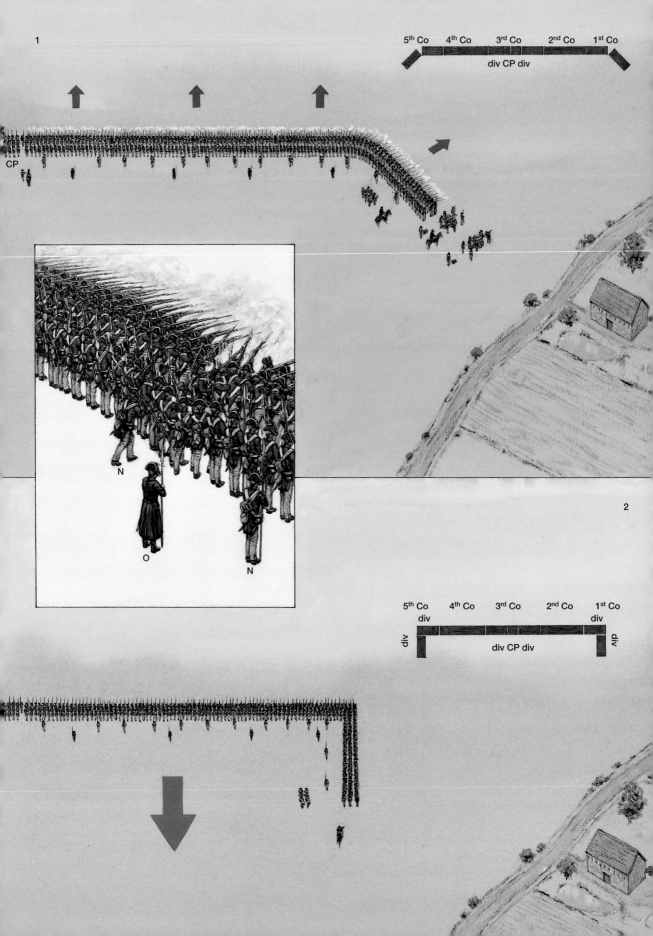

1

5th Co 4th Co 3rd Co 2nd Co 1st Co

div CP div

CP

N

O

N

2

5th Co 4th Co 3rd Co 2nd Co 1st Co
div   div

div   div

div CP div

them. Lieutenant von Schulenburg took a troop of 20 men from the 1st Squadron and charged the infantry frontally. This bold move cost the lives of one NCO and two men, but threw the enemy infantry into confusion. I then made a determined charge on them with two squadrons. They fought back bravely, but we nevertheless cut them about and rode them down. We pursued the enemy cavalry to the village of Rodemachern. The remnants of the enemy infantry that reached the wood were overthrown... The enemy lost 500 men. We captured 5 officers, 110 men and 42 horses.

This kind of 'war of outposts' was characteristic of the operations in the broken terrain of this theatre, and the Prussians, with commanders like Blücher, proved to be adept at it.

PIRMASENS

The first major battle in this theatre took place at Pirmasens on 14 September 1793. Here, a French force under Gen Moreau had attacked Prussian positions on 12 September, but was driven off by an artillery barrage. Since it was clear that the Prussians were determined to hold their ground, Moreau massed 12,000 men the next evening: 12 infantry battalions, three cavalry regiments, and 52 guns including battalion pieces. He marched them through the night on the road from Zweibrücken to Pirmasens, and reached Fehrbach, 1½ miles north-west of Pirmasens, at daybreak, thus by-passing fortifications on the heights south-west of the town (see map).

The Duke of Brunswick had anticipated such a manoeuvre, and had ordered his men to remain alert that night. This gave him the time to have Gen Kalckstein's division – 8 battalions, 10 squadrons and 2½ batteries – redeploy

Grenadier and officer of the Holstein-Beck Regt (IR No.11) in the uniforms of 1794. (Paintings by Bryan Fosten)

B | **MUSKETEER BATTALION IN 'CRESCENT', c. 1806**

Although the line was the optimum formation for maximizing infantry firepower, linear formations were particularly vulnerable to enemy cavalry – especially the flanks and rear of the line, which were largely defenceless. For this reason, infantry were instructed to adopt this formation when withdrawing in the face of the enemy.

By this date musketeer battalions had five companies; when in line, the colour party took post between the separated divisions of the central company.

1: When stationary, the division on each flank would be swung back at an angle of 45°.

2: When withdrawing, they would swing further back, perpendicular to the main line. This gave battalions the option of maintaining the line formation when withdrawing in the face of enemy cavalry, while delivering flank fires to discourage cavalry working their way around to the rear, instead of simply forming square – a largely immobile formation. Several withdrawing battalions could provide mutual support to each other.

Inset: The 'refused division' of a company in line giving fire.

Battle of Pirmasens,
14 September 1793. The French
attacked south-eastwards from
Fehrbach towards Pirmasens.
(Jany, *Geschichte*, vol iii, p. 272;
author's collection)

to the right and move onto the heights north-east of Pirmasens. He covered his right flank in the Ruppertwald with an infantry battalion, 160 Schützen and two heavy guns. The instant the French were sighted the Prussian artillery opened up. Hahn's horse half-battery advanced along the road to Fehrbach with a cavalry escort. Three more battalions of Prussians with 2½ batteries under Gen von Courbière moved up from Ketterich, while Kleist's brigade – 3½ battalions, 6 squadrons and 3 batteries – remained there to cover any French moves from that side.

A lengthy artillery bombardment began, but had little effect due to the long range. Moreau's tired and badly trained troops took a while to form three-deep columns, but at about 10 a.m. they started moving up on both sides of the road to Pirmasens. The right column, the vanguard under Gen Guillaume, consisted of 1,500 infantry and cavalry, while the other two were each 4,000 to 5,000 strong. Between the wooded Steinbach valley in the east and the Blümel valley in the west, the road crossed a ridge about 500 yards wide at the northern exit of Pirmasens. The French line of advance left its flanks open to the Prussian troops in the Ruppertwald and on the Huster ridge. The Prussian artillery, along with the battalion guns, opened fire on the left column. The Duke of Brunswick's Infantry Regiment then fired volleys by battalion at the French left column and drove it back, although the right column reached the town wall. The French cavalry chased off two squadrons of Prussian dragoons. Courbière's men then arrived, deploying facing north just south-west of the town. His artillery soon drove off the French, and by 1 p.m. they were in full flight, with the pursuing Prussian cavalry taking 13 guns. Of the 7,000 Prussians who saw combat, nine officers and 154 men were killed. The French lost 19 guns, and had 1,800 men taken prisoner; 800 dead were buried, but the number of wounded was unknown.

The briefest analysis thus shows that the Prussians took advantage of the terrain, covered their flanks with light and line troops supported by artillery, and then used their artillery to soften up the advancing French, before firing battalion volleys to drive them back, and pursuing with cavalry – in short, they made expert and co-ordinated use of all arms.

* * *

In the days following the battle of Pirmasens the Prussians pushed the French back to the Saar river. The Austrian field marshal Count Wurmser led the attack on Gen Moreau's major defensive lines at Wissembourg on 13 October 1793. Meanwhile, a Prussian force under Brunswick marched around the lines; this consisted of 9 battalions of infantry, 3 companies of Jägers, 15 squadrons of cavalry and 1½ horse batteries. Their line of approach was through narrow mountain passes between Pirmasens and Lembach, and was secured by small detachments. Once Moreau had fallen back to Strasbourg most of Brunswick's force rejoined Hohenlohe's, but a detachment consisting of a regiment of hussars, 2 fusilier battalions and 3 Jäger companies were left behind to cover the passes. They engaged in a war of outposts until mid-November, engaging the French forces occupying Landau; altogether, this month of operations demonstrated how adept the Prussian light forces were at moving and fighting in broken terrain.

The new commander of the French Army of the Moselle in the Palatinate, Gen Hoche, then advanced over a wide front from Saaralbern, Saargemünd and Saarbrücken towards Landau. On 17 November, Gen Count Kalckreuth fought a rearguard action at Biesingen, where his 7,000 to 8,000 men held up 20,000 Frenchmen. Six companies of Crousaz's Regiment threw back repeated French cavalry attacks while still in line.

During the night of 17 November the Prussians attempted to storm the French fort at Bitsch, to remove this obstruction from an important road. The storming party was assembled from detachments of 100 men each from various line battalions, along with two smaller groups of fusiliers. Armed with inside information about the defences from a French émigré, the storming party advanced under the cover of night in ten assault columns. The rocky cliffs on which the fort lay were scaled, and the palisade over the covered way was crossed. However, an attempt to blow up the gates to the tunnel failed, and, after four hours under small-arms fire and showers of grenades, stones and timbers, the stormers withdrew with heavy losses. Nevertheless, this small operation – conducted in darkness – demonstrates the ability of Prussian line infantrymen to fight effectively in detached parties even under the most demanding circumstances.

KAISERSLAUTERN

Shortly afterwards, the Prussian right-wing forces under the Duke of Brunswick marched to Kaiserslautern, where a concentration began on 25 November. A line of outposts secured the front and linked up with Hohenlohe's corps, whose left made contact with the Austrians at Wissembourg. The previous summer, Brunswick had seen to it that the fortifications at Kaiserslautern were strengthened. Earthworks were built on the western side of the ridge to the north of the town that runs down to the south-west, while one redoubt was constructed facing Moorlautern and another to the north of that village. A trench and abatis 2½ miles south-west of Kaiserslautern cut the road to Homburg, and a further trench cut the main road running west.

On 27 November, Hoche's Army of the Moselle approached the town, 36,000 strong. The right wing consisted of Gen Taponier's division, the left of Gen Ambert's, while Hoche commanded the main body. On the 28th, Taponier drove in the Prussian outposts. Finding the bridges across the Lauter river destroyed and the heights above them occupied, Hoche broke off the attack and camped for the night. Under the cover of darkness, he drew up 16 guns on the heights to the west of Kaiserslautern, within range of the plateau north of Moorlautern. The next morning, Ambert marched from Sambach to Otterberg to move against the eastern flank of the Prussians, but lost his way and went too far to the north-east. Hoche gained the heights north of the Otter stream, while the right moved up river along the Lauter valley.

The changing silhouette of
Prussian light troops over the
20 years of the Revolutionary
and Napoleonic Wars.
(Left) Bugler (hornist) of Fusilier
Bn von Rembow, 1792, clad
in 'hunter's green', faced
in this unit with pink.
(Centre) Private, Foot Jäger
Regt, 1806, in shorter green
coat faced and lined red.
(Right) Fusilier NCO, 1st West
Prussian Infantry Regt (No.6),
1814–15; the coatee is now
dark blue, faced here with
crimson, with gold NCOs'
lace at collar and cuffs.
The grey greatcoat is confined
in a horseshoe roll by a
buttoned leather sleeve.
Note that all have brass-
hilted sword-bayonets.
(Paintings by Bryan Fosten)

C FUSILIER BATTALION, c. 1806, WITH FLANK PLATOONS DEPLOYING AS SKIRMISHERS

The four-company battalion is drawn up in two ranks in conventional linear formation, with its officers **(O)** and senior NCOs **(N)** positioned much as in Plate A; note that fusiliers did not carry colours. Behind the battalion drummer, a reserve of 40 supernumeraries **(SN)** is drawn up at rear centre. The mounted commanding officer **(CO)** has sent forwards from the flanks the 1st and 8th 'Platoons' (in fusilier units, half-companies) to deploy as skirmishers; he waits with his bugler **(B)** on the crest of the first slope, where he is visible and can follow developments.

The two flank platoons halt behind the last cover – here, the foot of a second slope – before they reach the forward edge of battle. Supervised by the mounted 'skirmish captain' **(SC)** on the crest of the last slope, and led by their subalterns and NCOs, pairs of skirmishers peel off from the platoons and advance to form a firing line – those from the two platoons would link up in the centre. The remainder of the platoons wait behind in support. They can act either as rotating replacements for men in the skirmish line, or as a rallying-point if enemy cavalry drive the skirmishers back.

In 1806, the Prussian fusilier battalions operated independently of the musketeer battalions. Under the reforms of 1808 onwards one fusilier battalion was included within each infantry regiment, and thereafter the two fusilier battalions in a brigade were used to provide the skirmish element in the brigade's battle line. In 1806 there were already instances of flank companies and the third ranks of musketeer battalions being used as skirmishers. On such occasions they, too, would operate in two ranks, with pairs of skirmishers forming the firing line in front of formed reserves.

Inset 1: Each file formed a pair of skirmishers. The limitations of period firearms required that each man in a pair fired and reloaded in turn, so that one of them always had a loaded weapon. The NCOs did not take their place in a firing pair, but kept a watchful eye from just behind their squads of about ten men, ensuring that they made the best use of terrain and did not waste ammunition.

Inset 2: The fusilier company's two platoon officers were each accompanied by a bugler, to pass their orders by means of bugle-horn calls to the dispersed files of skirmishers.

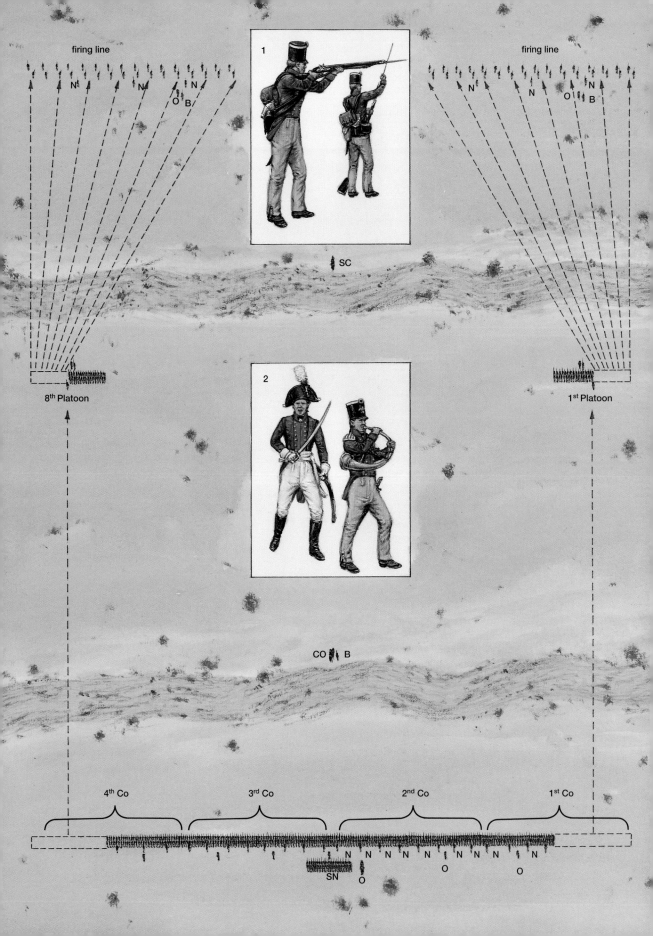

firing line

firing line

1

N   N   N
O   B

N   N   O   N
B

SC

2

8th Platoon

1st Platoon

CO   B

4th Co   3rd Co   2nd Co   1st Co

N N N N N N N N N N N
O   O   O

SN
O

Enfiladed by the French artillery and outnumbered by their infantry, the Prussians deployed along the southern bank of the Otter retired, allowing the French to cross it and deploy a battery on the plateau. This opened fire on the redoubt west of Erlenbach around midday, but the French largely overshot their targets; the Prussian artillery was better handled, and effectively enfiladed the French. At about 3 p.m. the French started to waver, so two regiments of Prussian cavalry ascended the plateau and charged them, driving them downhill into Erlenbach; one battalion tried to form square, but were cut down and taken prisoner.

French infantry then made a wild charge, reaching as far as the trench of the redoubt; but the Prussian infantry regiments of Kalckstein, Knobellsdorff and Brunswick confronted them, halted them with a series of battalion volleys, then closed on them with the bayonet and drove them back into the wood. A further French advance from the west of Erlenbach did not get far. Two Saxon and two Prussian cavalry regiments followed up; the French cavalry west of Erlenbach gained their flank, but the German troopers wheeled to the right and drove the French back.

General Ambert had found his way back, and hoped to try his flanking manoeuvre again the next day. At dawn on 30 November the artillery opened up, and four battalions of French infantry then advanced from Erlenbach towards the Bornberg hill to the south-east. General Kalckreuth counter-attacked with two battalions of Saxons and one of Guard grenadiers, who pushed the French back over the Otter stream. While he was doing this, a relief column under Gen von Kosporth arrived at the north of the battlefield, while Blücher's Red Hussars appeared in the rear of the French. On hearing that his artillery was running low on ammunition, Gen Hoche reluctantly withdrew his men across the Lauter. Brunswick then went over to the attack, his skirmishers covering the advance of his infantry and his cavalry supporting them; they reached the Lauter without resistance. Blücher's hussars, joined by the Life Cuirassiers, chased off several French cavalry regiments. News of Taponier's attack on the Duke of Weimar arrived:

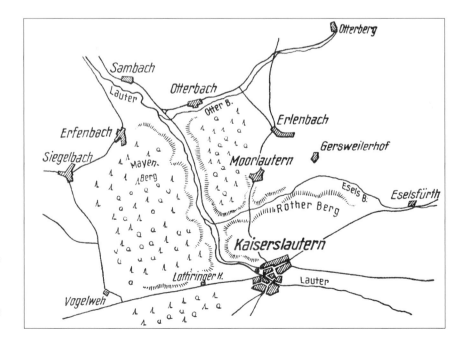

Battle of Kaiserslautern, 28–30 September 1793. The French advanced from the west towards the east and south. (Jany, *Geschichte*, vol 3, p. 277; author's collection)

the redoubt had withstood the attack, and although the left flank was driven back a counter-attack stabilized the situation, then drove the French back into the woods. In three days of fighting the Allies lost nearly 850 men, but the French more than 3,000, including 700 prisoners.

Minor skirmishes continued into the winter, but the Prussians were now getting war-weary; after two years spent defending the western border of Germany, funds were beginning to run low. Unrest in the newly-acquired Polish provinces was causing concern, so King Frederick William II was increasingly reluctant to squander any more of his limited resources in the west. Nevertheless, around 60,000 Prussian troops were committed to the Palatinate in 1794.

MÖLLENDORF IN THE PALATINATE

On leaving for Poland in spring 1794, the king left the command of the army on the Rhine in the hands of Field Marshal Möllendorf. Möllendorf's intention was to separate the two French armies in this theatre – the Army of the Rhine and the Army of the Moselle.

He began his movements in May 1794: leaving a force under Prince Hohenlohe to hold up the Army of the Rhine, he himself advanced on Kaiserslautern, intending to attack it on 23 May. A small detachment under Köhler – 4 battalions of infantry, the Trier Jägers, 5 cavalry squadrons and half a horse battery – joined Gen Kalckreuth's force (15 battalions, 25 squadrons, 3½ batteries), to cover the Prussian right and move on the French from the west. Meanwhile, Möllendorf led the main body from the north, leaving Gen Rüchel (7 battalions, 3 Jäger companies, 20 squadrons, 2½ batteries) to attack from the east. A detachment under Col Blücher moved along the road from Kaiserslautern to Neustadt to cut the line of communication between the two French armies. General von Courbière's force (4 Guards battalions, one heavy battery) remained in reserve.

General Ambert, commanding a single division at Kaiserslautern, saw the danger and withdrew to Pirmasens – mostly in good order, but the column panicked when its flanks were threatened, and the Prussian cavalry pressed home. Colonel L'Estocq's hussars alone took two colours, 13 guns and around 100 supply waggons, while the total French losses were about 1,800 prisoners, 6 colours and 17 guns. The Prussians lost only 110 dead, wounded and missing. Blücher's detachment fought off a number of attempts by French troops to break through. Ambert took the remnants of his force to Saargemünd, while Moreau withdrew his two divisions behind the Saar river; following up, Blücher took a further 6 guns, 2 colours and 300 prisoners on 28 May.

While the Allies were enjoying their successes on the middle Rhine, however, the French offensive into the Austrian Netherlands brought them victory

Gebhardt Leberecht von Blücher in c. 1800 as a lieutenant-general, and colonel-in-chief of his 8th Hussar Regiment, which he had led with distinction in the Revolutionary Wars. (Author's collection)

Line infantry musketeer and officer, Infantry Regt Rüchel (No.2), in 1806 campaign dress. (Paintings by Bryan Fosten)

at Fleurus on 26 June 1794, and subsequently control of the Rhineland. They could now move more men into the Palatinate, and again went over to the offensive there at the beginning of July. General Jourdan's advance from the Austrian Netherlands down the Rhine took Cologne, Andernach and Koblenz, and Möllendorf was forced to withdraw to the right bank of the river. On 1 October, the British subsidy upon which the Prussian war effort had depended ran out and was not renewed; and finally, the situation in Poland became more pressing. The Prussians signed a peace treaty with the French at Basle on 5 April 1795, withdrawing from the war, and remaining neutral for the next decade.

Prussia's withdrawal from the anti-French coalition was not due to any major defeat on the field of battle. On the contrary, the Prussians had fought well for as long as they had the funds to keep their army in the field. The actions described above support the judgement that the Prussians were always at least a match for the French tactically, and this was particularly true during the 'war of outposts' favoured by the broken terrain in the Palatinate. The Prussian senior commanders had led forces of all arms with skill, showing tactical flexibility in both the attack and the defence, and they withdrew from this war with both their army and their professional honour intact. They apparently had little to learn from what is often praised as the 'new, French method of warfare'.

D BATTALION IN COLUMN OF ATTACK PASSING THROUGH A DEFILE, 1812

From 1808 onwards the column of attack was the standard battlefield formation. A battalion of infantry again consisted of eight half-company divisions (see numbering), each of roughly 100 men; the divisions were aligned in pairs, with men drawn up in three ranks. The frontage of a battalion closed up in column was supposedly 50 paces. The battalion commander (CO) led from the front on horseback, flanked by a bugler (B) and a drummer (D) who could signal his orders. In the front ranks an officer marched on the outer flank of each division, with an NCO on the inner flank; the other subaltern officers and the remainder of the NCOs were spaced along behind the rear rank to ensure that order was maintained. The adjutant (A) rode at the rear of the battalion.

To pass through a defile – that is, between any terrain features that constricted the frontage – the men of the two leading divisions wheeled 90° to their left or right, then marched through in six parallel single files, with an officer (O) outside the head of each division, and the others and the NCOs (N) forming extra files between the divisions. As soon as the way was clear the other pairs of divisions turned successively and marched through the defile. The drummers (D), whose station in the column was behind the inner ends of the 3rd and 6th Divisions, completed the NCOs' files. On the far side of the defile, each pair of divisions in turn wheeled outwards to the left and right and faced front, thus re-forming the column of attack. The colour party remained in the lead throughout this manoeuvre, providing a point of reference.

The Prussian auxiliary corps that joined Napoleon's Grande Armée in Russia in 1812 amounted to three brigades, each of two regiments of infantry. These regiments generally consisted of three battalions drawn from various parent regiments – two of musketeers and one of fusiliers. The 1st Regiment included an additional battalion of fusiliers; and the East Prussian Jäger Battalion was attached to the 3rd Brigade.

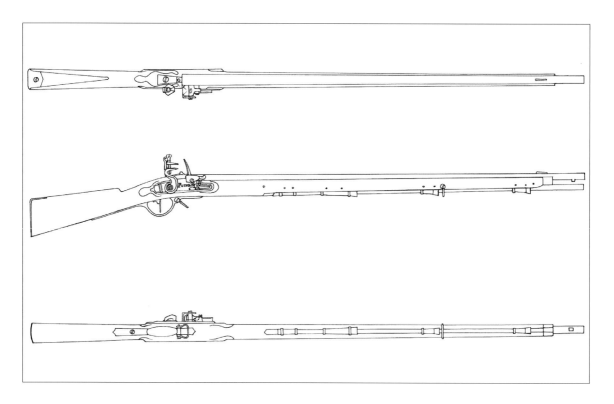

The Nothardt musket of 1801. Lack of funds and the outbreak of war in 1806 prevented its issue throughout the line infantry, and only a few Guard and other units received it. Its introduction was hampered by the logistic complication of its smaller calibre, preventing it taking ammunition manufactured for other patterns. Moreover, the 1813 trials showed that the 1801 pattern was, if anything, slightly less accurate than the old 1782 that was the standard issue up to and during the War of 1806. (By kind permission of Biblio-Verlag, Osnabrück)

THE TEN-YEAR PEACE

The Prussian infantry that fought in the Revolutionary Wars had been trained according to the 1788 Regulations – among the most modern of their time – and there appeared to be no immediate need for any radical changes. There had been no significant advances in weapons technology that required the battle-drills to be amended. The most effective way of using the muzzle-loading flintlock musket remained the deployment of the 'line' infantry in the very formation that gave them their name, so it is hardly surprising that the Prussian infantry were highly trained in linear evolutions. However, in the broken-terrain fighting in the Palatinate they had also employed other types of formation to suit combat situations; the Prussian fusilier regulations of February 1788 were one of the first produced anywhere specifically for light infantry, and were, as such, innovative. Governing the use of the skirmishers of both the line and the light infantry, they had proved their worth in the campaigns of 1792–95.

While war continued to rage in Europe, Prussian officers kept a close eye on developments. Although Prussia was at peace in the decade before Jena, it certainly was not asleep – indeed, if anything, too much attention was given to adjusting the regulations. The new cavalry drill regulations mentioned above were issued in 1796 – those for the cuirassiers and dragoons on 6 February, those for the hussars and Bosniaks on 25 June – and these, together with the Field Regulations of 1790, were the basis of the cavalry's training and battle-drills in 1806. However, as was common in the Prussian army at this time, each regional Inspection made its own amendments and modifications to the regulations, so it became necessary to virtually retrain any trooper transferred from one regiment to another.

Many of these Instructions (as the amendments to the regulations were termed) were issued locally, being restricted to one area or even one regiment. The first of these came out as early as 1791, when Duke Frederick William of Brunswick had an Instruction printed for his infantry regiment; at about the same time the Crown Prince produced one for his, and many others followed. In an attempt to put an end to the confusion, the recently crowned King Frederick William III published a large 'Instruction for Conformity in the Infantry' on 11 March 1798, which was the precursor for a planned general revision of the existing regulations, but little progress was made with the latter. Instead, from 1798 to 1805, the infantry was bombarded with amendments. These included the 'New Improved Instructions' of 14 October 1802, and on 30 December 1803 the 'Shortened and Improved Regulations for all Regiments and Battalions'. In addition to these amendments and regulations, there were a series of orders-in-cabinet and royal decrees on minor points.

THE COMMISSION FOR EXPERIMENTATION

This perhaps excessive fiddling was compounded by discussions on introducing a new infantry firearm, which was now at an experimental stage – the Nothardt, or 1801 pattern. Financial restraints put paid to a plan to equip the entire line infantry with this new musket; the units garrisoned in Potsdam were issued with it in October 1803, then the Guard in November 1805, but in all only seven battalions received it before the war of 1806. General von Rüchel headed up a 'Commission for Experimentation', which not only supervised the development of the new firearm but also considered changes in battle-drills to optimize its use. A substantial document on the subject was published in the form of an order-in-cabinet on 6 January 1801, followed on 6 August 1804 by a comprehensive regulation entitled 'Outline and Explanation of the New Movements and Orders when Loading Firearms'. All these publications were followed by memoranda explaining and expanding on them, to say nothing of the large number of privately published regulations at Inspection or unit level.

Particular attention was also paid to the growing use of light troops by the French army. It was evident that Prussia would need to increase its own skirmish elements, and to better integrate them with the line. While the fusilier battalions were highly regarded light infantry, and the rifle-armed Jägers were considered the élite of the élite, the small Schützen sections within the line battalions were insufficient in numbers. The need to increase the skirmishing capabilities of the line battalions led to various experiments, and a plethora of amendments to privately published regulations. For instance, in 1797 the Prince of Hohenlohe wrote a series of regulations for the Lower Silesian Inspection, which were published in 1803 under the title 'On the Use of the Third Rank as Skirmishers', and in 1805 the king ordered the general introduction of this tactic. The Prince Elector of Hesse (a Prussian field marshal, and Inspector-General of the Westphalian regiments) issued an order to his troops on 11 April 1806 instructing them to use not only the third rank as skirmishers, but where necessary entire companies, especially the flank companies.

It is clear that throughout this period of peace the Prussian army was paying considerable attention to developments in warfare, and was doing its utmost to modernize itself.

THE WAR OF 1806

So much for the theory; but was any of this put into practice? Paret, in his *Yorck and the Era of Prussian Reform* (1966), believes that 'Hohenlohe's experiment had no practical results'; but is he right?

Historians are fortunate indeed that it was the policy of the Prussian army for officers to produce after-action reports on the fighting in which they were involved, and that these reports were sent to the Historical Section of the Prussian General Staff – both as a record of events, and to form the basis for official histories of the campaigns, for the education of future generations of officers. Before we examine some of these reports, a glance at the organization and tactical drill of the army in 1806 is in order.

THE ARMY IN 1806

The 1788 Regulations were still in force, although with some modifications. The 1788 infantry regiment was to consist of one battalion of grenadiers and two of musketeers, each of four companies; but in 1799 King Frederick William III went back to the older method of raising only two companies of grenadiers from each line regiment, since raising four simply diluted the quality of what was supposed to be an élite element. Thereafter the paired companies from two regiments were used to form a combined four-company grenadier battalion. It was intended to increase the strength of each infantry regiment to three battalions to compensate for the loss of the grenadiers, and there was talk of incorporating one fusilier battalion to fulfil this role. The outbreak of war in 1806 prevented this, but the musketeer battalions were increased from

E **PRUSSIAN CAVALRY**

1: Liebertwolkwitz, 14 October 1813

This illustrates the tactical handling of Prussian cavalry (with a little Russian support) in this prelude to the decisive battle of Leipzig, 16–19 October. The cavalry combat went through several stages, including the initial deployment of the French IV Cavalry Corps against Russian hussars and Cossacks, and the intervention of Prussian cavalry reserves under MajGen von Röder, before the arrival of the Austrian IV Corps and cavalry decided that day's action.

The troops involved in the action shown here were, on the French side, the divisions of Milhaudt and Héritier, each consisting of five regiments of dragoons. The Prussian Reserve Cavalry of II Corps included the Silesian, East Prussian and Brandenburg cuirassier regiments. Sumy's Russian hussars, which had engaged the French at the beginning of the combat, were still disordered and re-forming to the rear, along with other Prussian cavalry regiments including the Neumark Dragoons and Silesian Uhlans. Two horse batteries provided support, the Prussian Horse Battery No.10 and the Russian Horse Battery Nikitin. At the stage depicted here, Mildhaudt's first two regiments – the 25e and 22e Dragons – have deployed into line, and his 20e, 19e and 18e Dragons are coming up in support, while Héritier is just starting to deploy from column of regiments. The three Prussian cuirassier regiments have wheeled to the left in line to face Milhaudt; the Silesians and East Prussians tied him down frontally, while

the Brandenburgers sought to gain his left flank. (For an account of the action of the Brandenburg Cuirassiers, see pages 54–57; and for further information on the whole campaign, see Campaign 25, *Leipzig 1813*).

Inset: A pair of Prussian dragoons skirmishing from the saddle; these are two of the 12 picked men per squadron issued with carbines. Even with the barrel resting on the raised left arm, firing from the saddle was inevitably inaccurate except at very close range. Carabineers carried the ramrod hanging down their chest, looped to a button.

2: Squadron in line formation

The captain led from front and centre. The squadron was subdivided into four *Züge* – troops or platoons (note numbering) – and drawn up in two ranks. Each troop was led from the front by a lieutenant (note seniority numbering), with one following at rear centre. The fifth ranking lieutenant was the *Fähnrich* or ensign, but in accordance with orders of 1 October 1811 the regiment carried only a single standard in the field, the *Leibfahne* of the 1st Squadron. The right marker in each troop's first rank was a *Flügelunteroffizier* ('wing' or flank NCO), and another closed the rank at the left of 4th Troop. Behind the rear rank rode *Schliessende Unteroffiziere* (file-closer sergeants). In addition to its 6 officers, 14 senior NCOs and 132 corporals and troopers the squadron had three trumpeters – note that they are positioned outside the rear rank of 1st Troop.

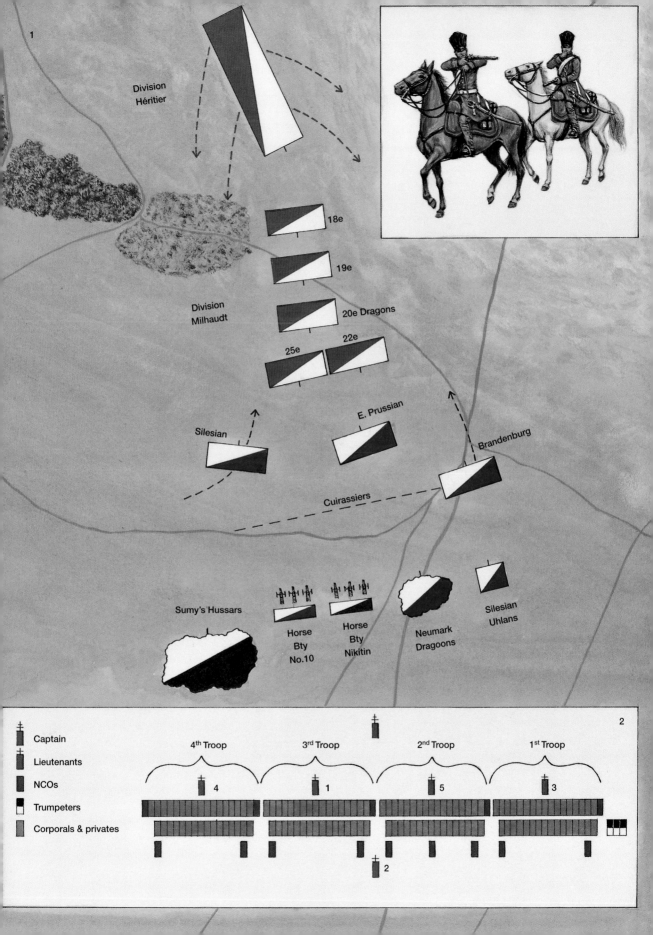

1

Division
Héritier

18e

19e

20e Dragons

25e 22e

Division
Milhaudt

Silesian

E. Prussian

Brandenburg

Cuirassiers

Sumy's Hussars

Horse
Bty
No.10

Horse
Bty
Nikitin

Neumark
Dragoons

Silesian
Uhlans

2

Captain

Lieutenants

NCOs

Trumpeters

Corporals & privates

4th Troop

3rd Troop

2nd Troop

1st Troop

4

1

5

3

2

four to five companies each. The line infantry available at the outbreak of hostilities consisted of the following units:

4 Guard battalions, each of 6 companies
28 grenadiers battalions, each of 4 companies
112 musketeer battalions, each of 5 companies

The light infantry consisted of:

24 fusilier battalions, each of 4 companies
Feldjäger Regiment (rifles) of 3 battalions, each of 4 companies

The battalion was the tactical unit in combat; regiments existed merely for administrative purposes. For grand tactical purposes the unit of manoeuvre was the brigade, assembled from a number of battalions.

In 1806, each regiment had a colonel-in-chief (*Chef*), who wore the uniform of a full colonel, but played no part in everyday duties, and a commander, who wore the uniform of a lieutenant-colonel. On the field of battle, the regimental commander now led the 1st Battalion, and a 'junior colonel' or lieutenant-colonel the 2nd Battalion. These battalion commanders handed their mounts over to their orderlies and marched with the colours, holding a spontoon; they stood in front of the colour party except when the unit was giving fire, when they stood behind them. Each regiment had three majors, and a supernumerary major. One of these rode behind each battalion; they and the ADCs/adjutants were the only officers who were mounted, and drew their swords on the field of battle. Since, from 1799, the regiments no longer had to provide a grenadier battalion commander, the third major took his place behind the right flank of

the 1st Battalion, and the supernumerary major behind the right flank of the 2nd Battalion.

Each musketeer battalion consisted of five companies, each of two divisions (*Züge*); each company consisting of 120 privates in the field and ten supernumeraries, giving each half-company division 20 three-man files, and a battalion in line 200 files. Each grenadier battalion consisted of only four companies, i.e. eight divisions, but as grenadier companies consisted of 150 privates (plus ten supernumeries) a grenadier division had 25 files and the battalion in line still had 200 files. Each battalion was to give priority to maintaining the width of its front, with losses to the front two ranks being made up with men from the third, as confirmed by an order-in-cabinet of 5 October 1805. The companies within a battalion were drawn up according to the seniority of their commanders, from both flanks towards the centre. Thus in a 1st Battalion they were drawn up, right to left, as follows: colonel's company, major's company, most junior captain's company, most senior captain's company, commander's company. In a 2nd Battalion the commander's company stood on the right flank, the major's on the left, and the three captains' companies between them, the most junior in the centre.

When the battalion formed up, the three ranks stood two paces apart from each other, with a line of NCOs and Schützen four paces to the rear of the third rank. The colour party (for details, see commentary to Plate A) initially stood five paces in front of the 6th Platoon, but aligned with it when the battalion closed up to fire. The company sergeant-majors stood in the centre of the battalion to guard the colours, and two files, each under an NCO, were now detailed as escorts on each side of the colour party. The divisional officers – the captain and first lieutenant – each stood on the right flank of their

(continued on page 36)

At Prenzlau, 28 October 1806, Murat's cavalry forced the Prussians under the Prince of Hohenlohe to capitulate. This impression of an engagement during the action shows French dragoons in combat with Prussian grenadiers in square. Although almost hidden by the powder-smoke, the front rank are visibly presenting bayonets while the rear two ranks fire – the standard Prussian drill when drawn up in square. (Richard Knötel; author's collection)

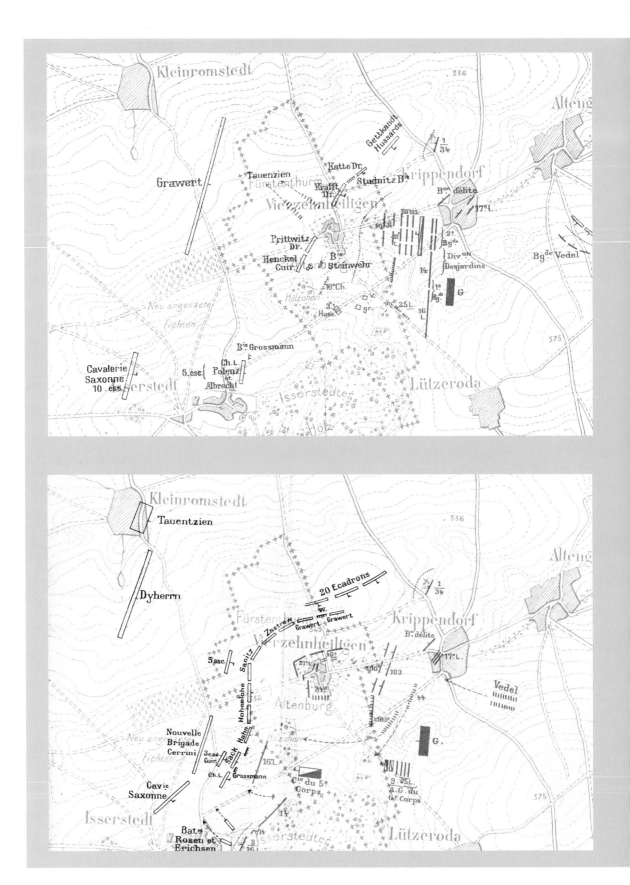

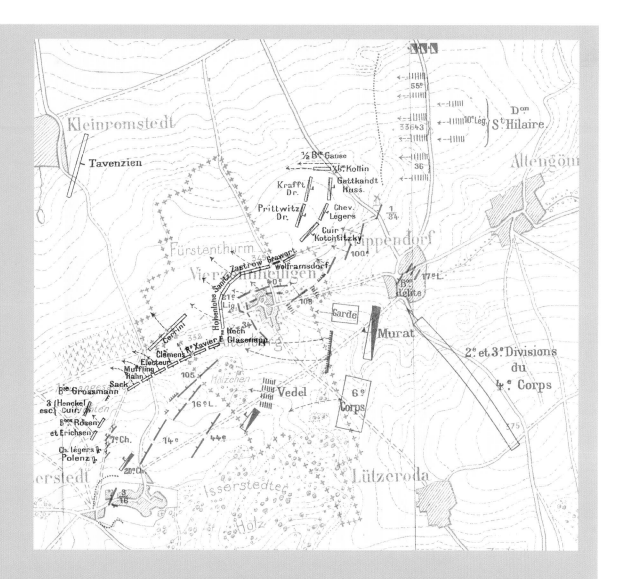

Part of the battlefield of Jena, 14 October 1806

ABOVE LEFT
Part of the battlefield of Jena, 14 October 1806: the situation around the villages north-west of the town at about 10 a.m – Prussians shown in blue, French in red. General Tauentzien's corps had already been driven back from his line stretching eastwards from Lützeroda, by the northwards thrust of Marshal Lannes' V Corps. Now his units were withdrawn, and Gen Grawert's division moved up towards Vierzehnheiligen. Both sides had been deployed in linear formations, but the French infantry then followed up in columns, since Prussian cavalry were operating behind them and they might need to form square rapidly. The heights of Closewitz – mentioned in Col von Kalckreuth's report quoted

in the text – are off this map section at lower right, due east of Lützeroda. (Bresonnet; author's collection)

LEFT
The same area of the Jena battlefield, about 11 a.m: Grawert attacks Vierzehheiligen, with his infantry battalions deployed in line – as were the French V Corps troops from Reille's Bde of Suchet's Div who were facing them in the open north and west of the village, and those from Gazan's Div waiting in reserve east of it. Prussian skirmishers were sent forwards into the woods on their right front, here south of the name 'Altenburg'. The 105th Ligne, 16th Légère and 14th Ligne from Desjardin's Div of Augerau's VII Corps had to be committed to clearing

them from the Altenburg Woods and Isserstedt Forest. (Bresonnet; author's collection)

ABOVE
By about 1 p.m. Napoleon had brought up massive reinforcements, which overwhelmed the Prussians. The entire Prussian infantry is deployed in line, but has no reserves available to fall back on. In these maps by the French General Staff historian, French infantry battalions engaging the Prussians are shown deployed in lines, while those in movement but not yet engaged are shown in column. This has contributed to a myth of French columns being tactically superior to Prussian lines. (Bresonnet; author's collection)

division, initially eight paces to the fore but then aligned with the front rank; the more junior 'closing' officers stood at the rear, two paces behind the line of NCOs and sharpshooters. The drummers formed two squads, one behind each flank company. A battalion took up this formation without further orders, as soon as it had loaded and shouldered its arms. Other than in training, a battalion only closed ranks when in the proximity of the enemy. In 1806, infantry battalions were of the following strengths:

	Grenadier	Musketeer	Fusilier
Officers	18	22–23	19
NCOs	56	60	48
Artillery officers	1	1	0
Surgeons	4	5	4
Drummers, incl. 1 bn or regtl drummer, oboist or bugler	12	15	5
Buglers	1	1	8
Fifers (Guard bns only)	8	0	0
Gunners (infantrymen)	17	17	0
Schützen	40	50	40
Privates	600	600	520
Supernumeraries	40	50	40
Artisans	8	10	8
Enlisted ranks (excl. art'y NCOs, & artisans)	774	793	661

The regimental gunners served the battalion pieces, each gun having a crew of eight. From 1796 all infantry regiments were equipped with light 6-pdrs, replacing the previous mixture of 3- and 6-pounders. The two battalion guns were commanded by an NCO detailed from the field artillery, who wore artillery uniform, while the gunners, being drawn from the battalion, wore their regimental uniform. (The fusiliers had been equipped with 3-pdrs, but an order-in-cabinet of 5 July 1806 abolished them.)

In 1806, there were 13 cuirassier regiments, 14 of dragoons, nine regiments and one battalion of hussars, and one regiment and one battalion of Towarczys (lancers, recruited in Prussian-occupied Poland, who replaced the former Bosniak corps). The cuirassiers and dragoons were both regarded as 'battle cavalry'. All the cuirassier regiments and 12 of the dragoon regiments had five squadrons, all the other cavalry regiments ten squadrons in two battalions. (The Prussian cavalry were the most feared and respected arm of service; shortly before Jena, Napoleon is reported to have warned Suchet that his infantry should fight them in square and with the bayonet.)

TACTICAL ASPECTS OF JENA AND AUERSTEDT

In 1806 the Prussian army suffered one of the most devastating defeats in its history, so it is natural to assume that it was simply not suited to the task in hand. Too often, historians generalize from a particular battlefield event, and ignore the broader picture. In fact, the Prussian tactics at Jena cannot have failed completely, since the army held off twice their numbers for eight hours, inflicting around 6,500 casualties on the French for 10,000 of their own. An

examination of the battle as a whole presents a totally different picture from that created by the comments of Elting, Chandler, Fuller *et al* quoted at the beginning of this text – a picture of the Prussian infantry standing around for hours, doing little other than presenting themselves as targets for the French *tirailleurs*, who supposedly won the battle. An examination of the facts, starting with the arrival of Grawert's division at 10 a.m., makes it possible to establish the full extent of any tactical failure.

At around 10 a.m., Grawert's and Holtzendorff's cavalry got into a prolonged fight with Ney's VI Corps cavalry at the head of his vanguard. This opening phase of the battle ended around 10.30 a.m. with both sides retiring, and Ney's infantry taking up positions from Vierzehnheiligen south through the Altenburg Woods and beyond. Prince Hohenlohe gave Grawert the signal to attack, and his division advanced against Vierzehnheiligen in echelon of two battalions, the left flank leading. Contrary to the claims of some historians, the Prussians deployed into lines 1,000 paces away from the French before even advancing, so they never had to deploy under fire. Colonel Hans Christoph von Kalckreuth, commander of Infantry Regiment Prince of Hohenlohe (No. 32) at Jena, wrote in his after-action report as follows:

> An impenetrable fog covered the horizon so that one could only see a few paces in front. The head of the column deploying was roughly towards Vierzehnheiligen, and when the final grenadier platoon of the right flank battalion had wheeled in this direction, the battalion halted, then marched off in line. The colours were moved to the fore and the entire line advanced around 1,200 to 1,500 paces, until ordered to halt just behind a small copse. While General von Grawert's division

Action at Altenzaun, 26 October 1806: an impression of Prussian fusiliers skirmishing. They are supervised by a mounted officer, and their supports wait under cover in the background, drawn up in close order – see our Plate C. At Altenzaun, Col Johann von Yorck – one of the most influential figures in the development of the Prussian light troops – commanded the Prussian rearguard of Jägers and fusiliers, and held up the French advance long enough for the main body of the Prussian army to withdraw over the Elbe river. (Richard Knötel; author's collection)

carried out this manoeuvre, on the left flank of the Corps the brigades of General von Sanitz and General von Tauentzien were very heavily engaged with the enemy. After a short pause, we were ordered to move closer to the enemy. We moved off again, and part of the regiment passed by a [clump of bushes] in front of us. As we were to advance in echelon, each battalion wheeled to the left by about 40 paces and formed one echelon, with the entire line advancing [in the direction of] the enemy position on the heights of Closewitz until within artillery range, and halted under artillery fire while the echelons formed into a single line. During this manoeuvre, the enemy artillery killed and wounded a number of members of the regiment.

Suchet's division of Lannes' V Corps then moved up against Vierzehnheiligen, in echelon leading with the right – a mirror of the Prussian advance. During that advance, in front of Vierzehnheiligen the vanguard and the tirailleurs avoided the shock of the Prussian infantry by falling back into the village and the woods. Colonel Kalckreuth's report continued:

Close to the position the regiment was now holding, in front of us on our right was the extensive Isserstedt Forest, and [further to the] left a smaller wood. Both were held by large numbers of enemy skirmishers. Those in the wood on the left were very quickly driven out by the regiment's Schützen, but the Isserstedt Forest could not be entirely cleared of the enemy, since the forest extended as far as the enemy's position.

Major von Lessel, of Holtzendorff's detachment, added that 'As the Schützen could not drive the tirailleurs out of the wood, General von Sanitz had reserves formed from the third rank of the units, and threw them into the wood too.' (This is a clear example of the third rank being employed in a skirmish function.) On the Prussian right, Rosen's and Erichsen's fusilier battalions, Jägers, volunteers, and Schützen from the other line battalions participated in this action, pursuing a battalion of the 25th Légère to the eastern edge of the forest, where the Prussians halted – because going any further would have brought them deep within the French lines. A battalion of French grenadiers and the rest of the 25th Légère in the Altenburg Woods had held their ground with great difficulty in front of Grawert's right-flank battalions, but finally began to withdraw. Again, the Schützen and volunteers of Hohenlohe's battalions facing the Altenburg Woods pushed the French out of them. This was the first Prussian tactical success in the battle of Jena.

The Prussian artillery then opened fire, forcing the grenadiers, 25th Légère and Ney's artillery to withdraw further, thus obliging the vanguard of Ney's VI Corps to evacuate the Issertstedt Forest as well as the smaller Altenburg Woods. This Prussian success forced Napoleon to order the 16th Légère, from Desjardins' division of Augereau's VII Corps, to remove the Prussian skirmishers controlling the wood to the left of the division, and to take over the line evacuated by Ney. Desjardin's 14th and 105th Ligne were also ordered to enter Isserstedt Forest and Altenburg Woods. Shortly after 10.30 a.m. four French battalions entered the woodlands, but did not regain control of them for about an hour.

Meanwhile, the remaining infantry of Grawert's division marched to attack Vierzehnheiligen village. The French grand battery of more than 30 guns was

drawn up behind the Altenburg Woods and the village, but was masked by the slopes until Sanitz's Regiment came within sight of it. The artillery fire, combined with the fire of the French tirailleurs in the open and in the village, caused Sanitz's Regiment to fall back, forcing Hohenlohe to halt the division while he restored order. Hohenlohe then deployed a line of skirmishers in front of the village, but these were too few to make any impression. A Prussian 12-pdr battery was then brought up, and inflicted serious damage on the French artillery; another Prussian battery shelled the village and set it on fire. It was at this point that the events occurred that have caused the myth of the Prussian battalions standing aimlessly under fire.

There was indeed a pause in the Prussian assault on Vierzehnheiligen, during which French tirailleurs fired on the Prussian battalions halted in front of them close to the village. Nevertheless, Hohenlohe then resumed his advance on Vierzehnheiligen. Marshal Lannes, commanding the French V Corps, noted in his report that the volley fire of the Prussians was intense and terrible, and that this was 'the most critical [moment] of the day'. Suchet's division of V Corps suffered 24 per cent losses that day, largely due to Prussian small-arms fire. This was the second Prussian tactical success at Jena.

Lannes then ordered a spoiling attack on the Prussian left flank by the 100th and 103rd Ligne from Gazan's division. This attack was repulsed, though with difficulty; and the intensity of French fire from inside Vierzehnheiligen seemed to diminish, partly due to the blaze started by the Prussian shelling. This was the third Prussian tactical success.

The Prussian second line, consisting of Cerrini's fresh brigade, then reinforced the main line on the right, between Hohenlohe's Regiment and Hahn and Sack's grenadier battalions. Hohenlohe once again resumed his advance on Vierzehnheiligen, intent on having several battalions take the village with the bayonet. On learning of this intention, Grawert persuaded him to wait for Gen Rüchel's detached corps to arrive; but Rüchel took longer than anticipated, and by then Napoleon had brought up strong reinforcements. At around midday Napoleon ordered a general advance, and before long the Prussians were overwhelmed by weight of numbers.

The facts thus conflict with the facile myth of the Prussians merely standing around while being shot to pieces by French tirailleurs. The French skirmishers certainly did do serious damage, but the Prussians were only motionless targets in two specific instances: after Sanitz's Regiment was forced back, and while waiting to fight off Lannes' spoiling attack later. Nowhere was it the intention of the Prussian generals simply to stand and deliver volleys, and for all their tactical errors and lack of decisiveness their regiments achieved far more than that. The Prussians did not lose the battle of Jena due to the casualties caused by French skirmishers, anymore than they lost due to the French artillery. Grawert's division – which was only one of the six Prussian divisions fighting at Jena – cleared the woods to their front of French tirailleurs, and fought off two attacks by the French. The following conclusions are clear:

(1) The outnumbered Prussians were unable to deploy sufficient skirmishers to gain the upper hand over the French tirailleurs; but they did deploy about 25 per cent of their entire infantry as skirmishers, which was normal for the period.

(2) Their three arms – infantry, cavalry and artillery – basically fought separate battles. This lack of co-ordination by senior Prussian officers – who had not seen action in a decade – contrasts with the more skilful manner in which the experienced French generals handled their troops.

(3) The Prussians were outnumbered and outfought, and were crushed during their retreat; but on the field of battle they gave a good account of themselves. They fought for eight hours while outnumbered 2:1 at every point, and still achieved a number of tactical successes. This hardly suggests that the French battle-drills were superior to the Prussian; in each case, the Prussians' local successes were achieved by using very 'un-Frederickian' tactics.

The greatest mistake the Prussians made at Jena was not in using 'outdated' battle-drills, but in fighting the battle in the first place; given their disadvantages of both numbers and terrain, they would have been wiser to engage in a holding action while making an orderly withdrawal.

AUERSTEDT

Meanwhile, up the road at Auerstedt, the Prussians enjoyed superiority in numbers, but for various reasons did not make good use of them. These reasons included Davout's skilful tactical handling of a situation in which all he had to do was stay put in the morning fog and hold his ground, while the same fog caused the Prussian advance to fall into confusion. Finally, he profited from a lack of proper battlefield management by the Prussians, due in part to the mortal wounding of their commander-in-chief, Duke Carl William Ferdinand of Brunswick. The report of Col Carl Christian von Elsner of the Duke of Brunswick's Infantry Regiment (No. 21) makes this clear:

> Our approach march to the battlefield was made in good order, although it was too far to the right. We had no idea whatsoever of the

enemy's dispositions or positions, nor any knowledge of the terrain. Large gaps opened up between the battalions and regiments... When the battalion deployed on the ridge on the other side [of the village of Rehhausen] I finally saw the enemy's positions, and we wheeled a quarter to the left to face an enemy square. We continued our advance through battalions that had already been driven back, and battalions advancing on the left, and joined in with these unco-ordinated attacks, which achieved nothing.

Other after-action reports confirm that, where necessary, Prussian infantry were deployed in skirmish order, as Col von Raumer of Infantry Regiment No.28 recorded: 'On 14 October at daybreak, all the regiment's Schützen, along with a squadron of the Queen's Dragoon Regiment, were assigned to the command of Adjutant-General von Pfuhl to form a patrol... and unfortunately the regiment had to fight the entire battle without its Schützen... due to this lack of Schützen, the left flank company of the battalion was used for that purpose.' This is one good example of using a flank company to skirmish, and there are many more. Indeed, when the Duke of Brunswick was mortally wounded at Auerstedt he was leading the skirmish section of Hanstein's Grenadier Battalion towards the heights dominating the village of Hassenhausen, after having called up the skirmish sections of the other battalions of Wartensleben's division.

The cavalry too enjoyed local successes at Auerstedt, as shown by LtCol Frederick Ludwig von Jagow's report on the role of Irwing's Dragoon Regiment:

By now, the Dragoon Regiment had reached the assigned position along the road on the enemy's flank. It wheeled towards them and, saying 'Now's the time to go for them', I ordered it to attack... We advanced quickly and without hesitation towards the line of enemy infantry about 400 to 500 paces away, and into their left flank and rear. As we closed in on them the Schützen of Krafft's Grenadier Battalion fired continuously into their flank. Irwing's Regiment split up their entire left flank, consisting of four battalions [12th and 85th Ligne, each of two battalions, from Gudin's division], cutting down the fleeing and scattered enemy, a number of whom threw away their firearms.

Let us also not forget that Gudin's division, part of Davout's corps, suffered a staggering 42 per cent casualties in the fighting around Hassenhausen. That is an indication of how effective the 'worst musket in Europe' actually was, and how the 'parade-ground façade' of the 'hopelessly outdated' Prussian infantry actually performed in close combat. In case any doubt remains as to the suitability of the Prussian battle-drills, the last word goes to Pascal Bressonnet, the French General Staff historian of 1806, who commented that 'The elementary tactics used by the Prussians were thus sufficient to be measured against our own.'

THE LATER REFORMS, 1807–15

One of the conditions of the Peace of Tilsit signed between France and Prussia in 1807 reduced the Prussian army from the 200,000 men of 1806

ABOVE

A battalion in line, drawn up in three ranks, according to the 1812 Regulations.

The companies are drawn up with the 1st on the right flank through to the 4th on the left. The company captains stood on the right of their companies, the first lieutenants on the right of their divisions, and the others behind the companies, just to the rear of a line of NCOs.

The major commanding the battalion led from the front, ahead of the colour party, accompanied by two musicians to relay his orders. The rest of the musicians, the battalion drummer and the major's aide/adjutant took post behind the battalion. This formation was essentially unchanged since the 1790s – see our Plate A. (Hartwig, *Elementar-Taktik*; author's collection)

BELOW

However, the preferred attack formation had now changed dramatically to this battalion 'in column of attack by the centre'. The officers are marked in red, the NCOs in dark blue, the rank-and-file in light blue. The musicians are in the centre of the column, with the drummers to the left and the buglers to the right. (Hartwig, *Elementar-Taktik*; author's collection)

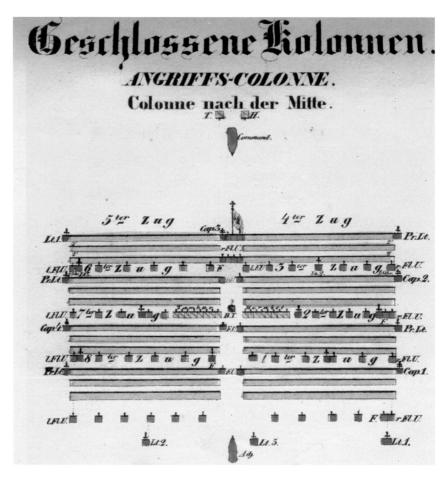

to a mere 42,000. Massive reparations were also imposed, pushing Prussia to the brink of bankruptcy in the years that followed. The lack of funds and the restricted size of the army were the two primary issues facing the new government. Furthermore, thanks to a substantial reduction in the size of Prussian territory, the system of local conscription would have to be entirely reorganized. The army reforms already under way in 1806 were continued, but were greatly affected by the restraints on funding and manpower.

For instance, in November 1806 the number of Schützen in each line company was increased to 20, but the whole practice was soon abandoned, and thereafter the third-rank men provided the basic skirmishing force for the battalion. (In March 1809 a complete unit, the Silesian Schützen Battalion, was formed, and in June 1814 a Guard Schützen Battalion.)

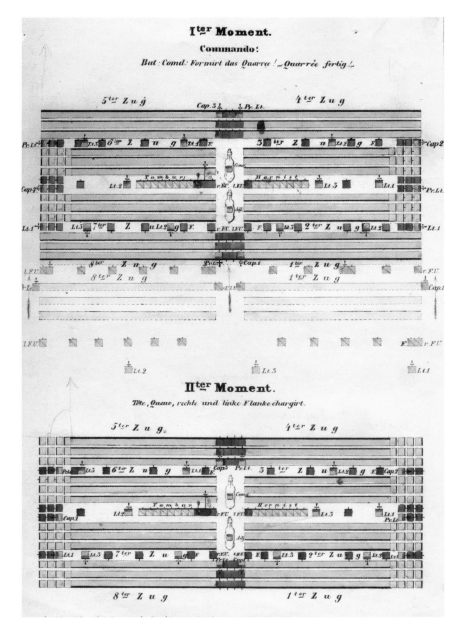

The formation of a 'square' from a column took place in two movements. In the first (top), the intervals between the ranks and divisions were closed, and the four flank files of the centre divisions turned to face the outside of the square. In the second movement, the remaining four flank files turned to face the outside, and officers moved from the front to the rear of the files – see our Plate G2. Under the 1812 *Exerzir-Reglement*, square was always formed from column; a unit that was deployed in line would have to form a column first. (Hartwig, *Elementar-Taktik*; author's collection)

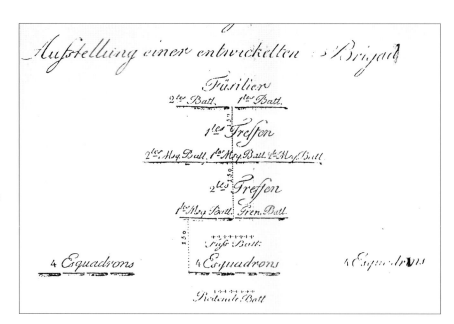

THE 1812 INFANTRY REGULATIONS

The first major reform planned had been the introduction of permanent all-arms divisions and corps, but under the circumstances this could not be properly implemented. Instead, permanent brigades of mixed arms were established. Once that was done the necessary drill regulations were drafted; these went through various editions, until the 1812 Regulations were adopted. These introduced two main novelties: firstly, an emphasis on the

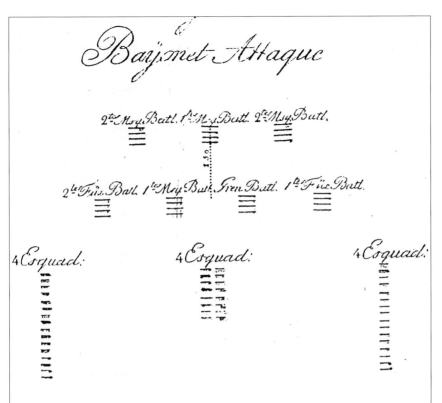

Banjmet Attaque

2⁜ Msq Batl. 1⁜ Msq Batl. 2⁜ Msq Batl.

2⁜ Füs. Batl. 1⁜ Msq Batl. Gren Batl. 1⁜ Füs. Batl.

4 Esquad: 4 Esquad: 4 Esquad:

LEFT
When moving towards contact with the enemy, the skirmishers fell back on their main body and the fusilier battalions then formed up in column on either flank of the second wave of infantry. The cavalry remained in reserve, while the artillery was deployed according to circumstances.
(Author's collection)

BELOW
When attack by enemy cavalry was imminent, the fusilier battalions moved forwards into the first line to create a symmetrical chequerboard pattern, and all the infantry battalions would form close squares from column, while cavalry moved up the flanks to cover them – see our Plate G1.
(Author's collection)

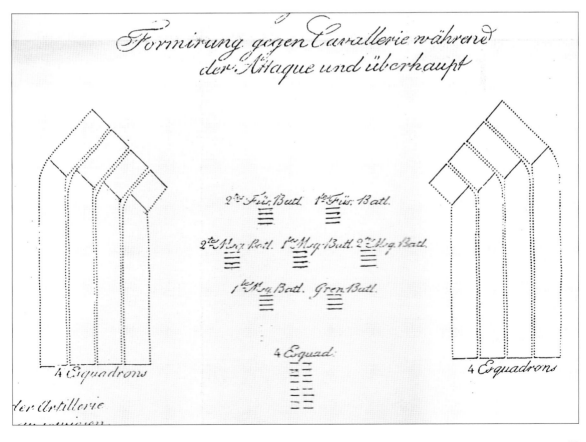

Formirung gegen Cavallerie während der Attaque und überhaupt

2⁜ Füs. Batl. 1⁜ Füs. Batl.

2⁜ Msq Batl. 1⁜ Msq Batl. 2⁜ Msq Batl.

1⁜ Msq Batl. Gren Batl.

4 Esquad:

4 Esquadrons   4 Esquadrons

der Artillerie

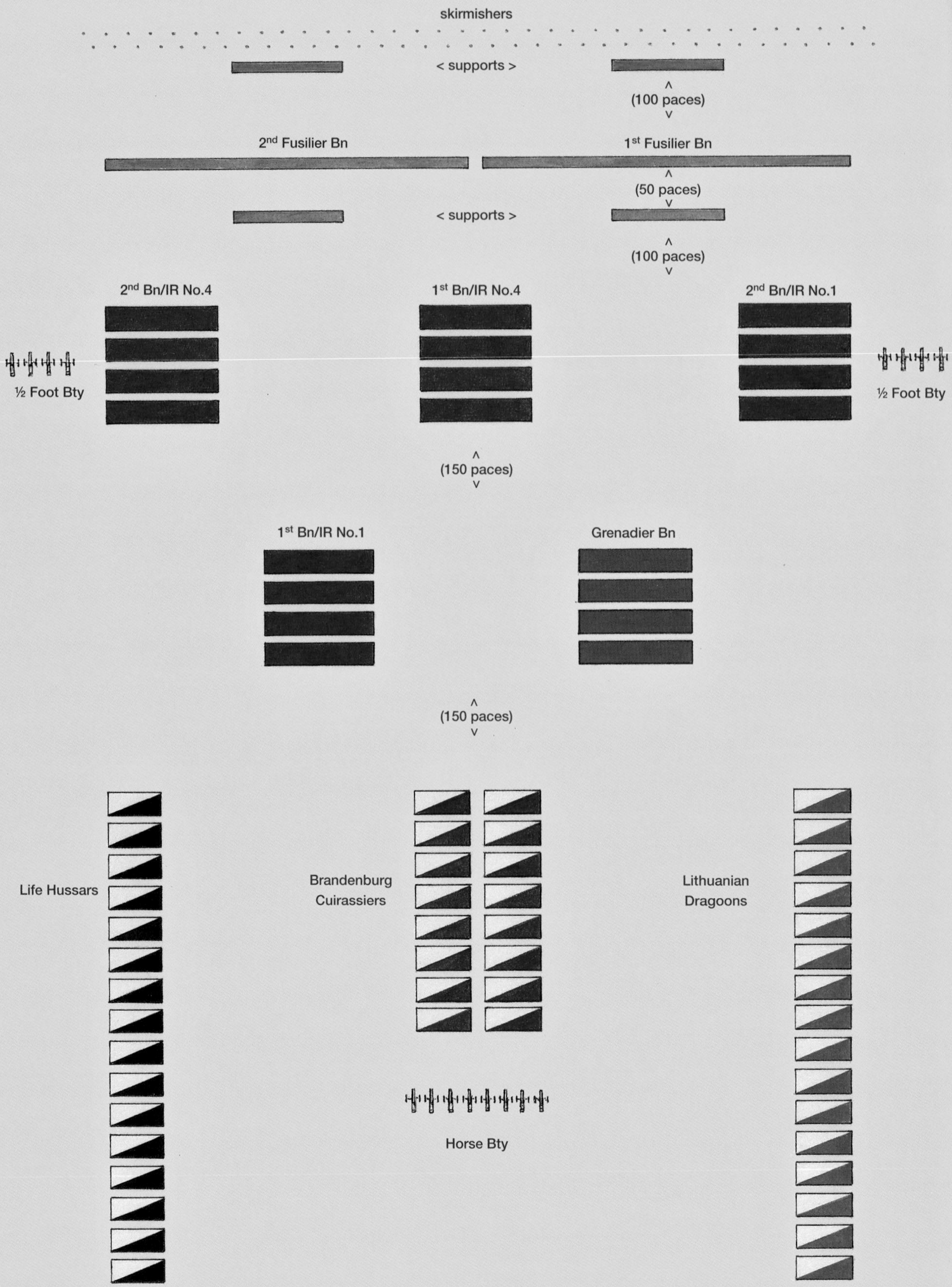

skirmishers

< supports >

∧
(100 paces)
∨

2nd Fusilier Bn

1st Fusilier Bn

∧
(50 paces)
∨

< supports >

∧
(100 paces)
∨

2nd Bn/IR No.4

1st Bn/IR No.4

2nd Bn/IR No.1

½ Foot Bty

½ Foot Bty

∧
(150 paces)
∨

1st Bn/IR No.1

Grenadier Bn

∧
(150 paces)
∨

Life Hussars

Brandenburg
Cuirassiers

Lithuanian
Dragoons

Horse Bty

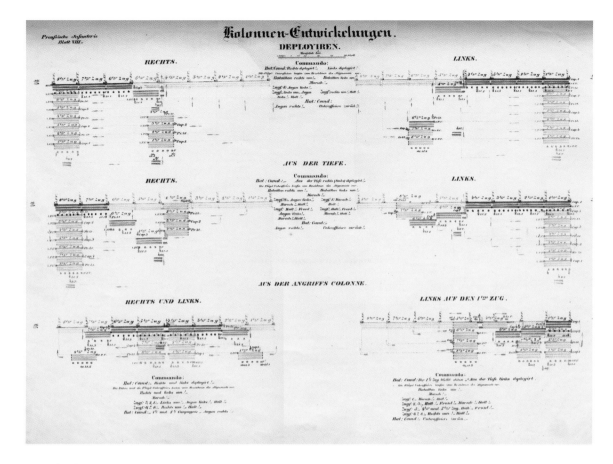

Here the various methods of forming line from column are shown – in the top two examples, from a column of divisions, and in the bottom image, from a column of attack. (Hartwig, *Elementar-Taktik*; author's collection)

use of infantry battalions in columns instead of the lines previously favoured, and secondly, the regulation of all-arms combats. The former was a concession to the decline in the level of training of the infantry and the dilution in the quality of manpower; it was easier to train men to fight in column than in line.

The basic foot drill stipulated in 1812 was essentially unchanged. The '*Ordinairschritt*' or slow pace of 75 paces per minute was used when training

F EAST PRUSSIAN BRIGADE IN ATTACK FORMATION (1812 REGULATIONS)

The favoured time to practise manoeuvres was the autumn; the crops had been harvested, leaving large stretches of land under stubble where the troops could march and counter-march without causing loss to Prussian farmers. Moreover, since the available manpower was no longer needed for agricultural work, men on furlough could be called up without disrupting the local economy.

The 1812 Regulations required Prussian brigades to adopt a 'chequerboard' formation of infantry battalions, with each formed in column of attack, and each wave of the brigade providing support to the others. The two fusilier battalions formed the vanguard; the majority of their troops formed a single two-deep line, while sub-units deployed forwards into a skirmishing line formed by pairs of men (see Plate C), with

small supporting parties in line 50 paces behind. A hundred paces behind these came three musketeer battalions in column: from left to right, the 2nd and 1st Battalions of the brigade's junior regiment (3rd E. Prussian IR, No.4), and the 2nd Battalion of the senior regiment (1st E. Prussian IR, No.1). An interval of 150 paces separated these from the 1st Battalion of the senior musketeer regiment, together with the battalion formed from the grenadier companies of both the brigade's regiments (1st E. Prussian Grenadier Battalion).

Following another 150 paces behind, the cavalry regiments of the brigade were normally kept in reserve to the rear. Here, we show the Life Hussars on the left and the Lithuanian Dragoons on the right, both in 'column of troops', flanking the Brandenburg Cuirassiers in 'column by the centre' – i.e., with the 16 troops in eight side-by-side pairs. The artillery was deployed according to circumstances.

and for parades. The '*Geschwindschritt*' or fast pace of 108 paces was used on most occasions, and was accelerated to 120 paces when charging; short distances could be covered at the trot, and the pace was given by drumbeats. Arms drill was simplified; firing was either by volley or by file, the orders again being passed by drum. Only the first two ranks fired, from the standing position. When in square, the first rank adopted a defensive stance with out-thrust bayonets, while the second gave fire, and the third reloaded and passed the loaded weapons forwards.

A four-company infantry battalion drew up with its eight half-company divisions each in three ranks. The basic formation was the '*Colonne nach der Mitte*', or open column of divisions 'by the centre'. Here the divisions were placed in four pairs behind one another; the 4th (right) and 5th (left) Divisions, with the colour party between them, together formed the first of the four triple lines. This 'attack column' was employed not only for attacking, but also for retiring – particularly when under threat of pursuit by cavalry, as the rank-and-file could be closed up quickly to form an almost solid 'square' (see Plate G2). Despite the fact that such a mass of men presented a better target for enemy artillery than a line, the column remained the favoured battlefield formation in the wars of 1813–15.

Post-Jena, the fusilier battalions still carried out special duties – skirmishing, forming vanguards, rearguards, outposts, etc. – and each company was expected to be able to fight in divisions (i.e. quarter-companies) two ranks deep when skirmishing. The third rank of the grenadier and musketeer battalions were also designated as skirmishers, selected from the most suitable recruits and given the best muskets. A specially designated 'skirmish captain' commanded the four skirmish elements formed from the third ranks of the companies. The 1809 Instruction had stated that 'the best light infantryman is the least mechanical man. When training for skirmish actions, all formal drill must be left behind.' The reality was somewhat different, since scattered lines of men armed only with single-shot weapons were vulnerable, and dependent on their closed-order supports. Because of command and control issues, only the minimum necessary numbers would be deployed as skirmishers, as determined by the terrain and enemy strength. Skirmishers could never decide a battle; they could only open it, and cover the movements of the closed-order troops, whose attack would decide the outcome. In the latter part of the Napoleonic Wars the Prussian infantry fought in depth, feeding the skirmish line until the decisive moment. Consequently, these were more drawn-out affairs than a Frederickian battle.

BRIGADES

Each infantry regiment included two battalions of musketeers, one of fusiliers, and two companies of grenadiers, the latter being detached and combined in one battalion at brigade level. The cavalry consisted of cuirassiers, dragoons, hussars and Uhlans (lancers, formed from 1809), each regiment having four squadrons. The artillery foot and horse batteries normally had six 6-pdrs and two 7lb howitzers, and the heavy foot batteries six 12-pdrs with two 10lb howitzers. A brigade consisted of two infantry regiments (i.e. seven battalions – four musketeer, two fusilier, one grenadier), three cavalry regiments, and a foot and a horse battery. A total of six brigades were formed, one each in East Prussia, West Prussia, Brandenburg, Pomerania, Lower Silesia and Upper Silesia. The brigades were trained to fight in four different modes: deployed, attack formation, bayonet charge, and defence against cavalry.

When deployed in line, the fusilier battalions were to the fore, three musketeer battalions in the first main line, the senior musketeer battalion (1st Bn of the senior regiment) and the grenadier battalion in the second line, with the foot battery to their rear. Behind them, the 12 cavalry squadrons were drawn up in one line, with the horse battery to their rear.

When in attack formation (see our Plate F), a fusilier skirmish line with supports deployed to the front of the brigade, with the main body of the fusilier battalions in line behind them. Behind these, the main wave consisted of three battalions of musketeers in column, with half the foot battery on each flank. The columns of the senior musketeer and the grenadier battalion were in reserve, 150 paces further back. The three cavalry regiments in column, and the horse battery, remained behind the infantry.

When closing to meet with the enemy, the fusilier battalions fell back to the main force and reformed in columns, one on each flank. The infantry then advanced in two waves: one of three musketeer battalions, the other of the two fusilier battalions, the senior musketeer and the grenadier battalion (see page 45, top). The cavalry followed the infantry.

When expecting attack by cavalry (see our Plate G1), the brigade formed a tighter chequerboard formation, with the fusiliers in front, three musketeer

(continued on page 52)

The modernized appearance of Prussian regular line infantry in 1812–13, exemplified by a musketeer and NCO of the 2nd Silesian Infantry (IR No.12) in campaign dress. The private has a white circle painted as a national cockade on his black oilskin shako-cover – at this date the Prussians were providing a national contingent to the Grande Armée. His grey greatcoat has regimental distinctions – a yellow collar and red shoulder straps. These are also applied to the sergeant's short dark blue coatee; note on his uncovered shako the brass plate, cockade, and gold rank lace at the top, and his laced collar and cuffs. Only a minority of the Army of the Lower Rhine in 1815 would be as completely uniformed and equipped as these regulars of the as-yet unexpanded army. (Paintings by Bryan Fosten)

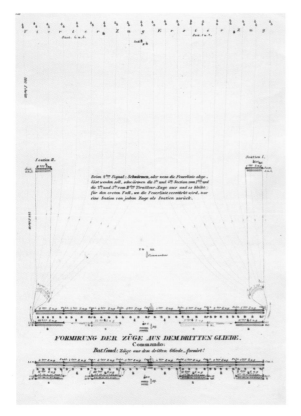

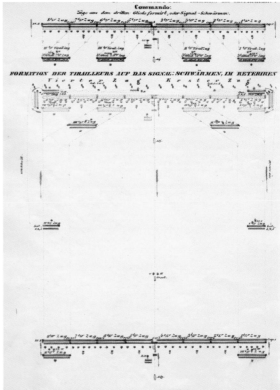

LEFT

How a skirmish line was formed by a line infantry unit. The first stage (bottom) was to form the skirmish divisions from the men of the third rank of the battalion, who formed up to the rear of the unit in two ranks. In the second stage, the 3rd and 4th sections of the 1st skirmish division, and the 2nd and 3rd sections of the 4th division, deployed as skirmishers; the remainder were held in reserve as supports. (Both Hartwig, *Elementar-Taktik*; author's collection)

RIGHT

Skirmishers could also be deployed when a unit was withdrawing. The skirmish divisions would form up to the rear of the battalion, which would then pass through the skirmish divisions before they deployed into skirmish order.

G | EAST PRUSSIAN BRIGADE DEPLOYED TO MEET CAVALRY (1812 REGULATIONS)

1: Brigade deployment, from formation shown on Plate F

First, the two fusilier battalions have re-formed into attack columns in the first wave of the brigade, while the musketeer and grenadier battalions, already in column, have closed up to form 'squares' (see below). They have adopted a tighter diamond-shaped 'chequerboard' formation, so that each can deliver enfilade fire along the faces of adjoining squares. The brigade's two light cavalry regiments, on the rear flanks, have deployed from column of troops into line of squadrons, and are sweeping forwards around the flanks of the infantry to meet the enemy cavalry; the heavy cavalry regiment has retained its position at rear centre, as a reserve ready to deploy and intervene depending upon events.

2: Battalion 'square' formation, after Hartwig

The use of 'crescents' and open squares fell out of favour when the battalion column became the favoured formation post-1808. All that needed to be done to turn a column into a solid square (actually, a rectangle) was to close ranks, face the flanking files outwards, and make some other minor adjustments. This could be achieved quickly and simply, and gave protection against cavalry without sacrificing mobility.

The eight divisions are still in the same relative positions (see numbering). The 1st, 2nd, 7th and 8th Divisions have about-faced. The four flanking files of each division have turned 90 degrees right or left to face outwards, as have some of the officers and NCOs filling the gaps between the divisions. Ten NCOs and two officers form a plug in the centre of both the front and rear pairs of divisions; the remainder keep their conventional posts behind the rear rank of their divisions. The commanding officer (**CO**) and his adjutant (**A**) remain in the saddle in the centre of the formation; flanking them are the drummers, and the colour party.

Inset: Positions in part of the right outer face, as marked.

Top, the outer five files of the rear rank of the 3rd Division, with the outer four files turned 90 degrees right; the front-rank man is in the 'charge arms' position, while the two behind him prepare to give fire.

Centre and below, the two ranks filling the gap between the 3rd and 2nd Divisions, formed by three NCOs of the former, and the first lieutenant and two NCOs of the latter.

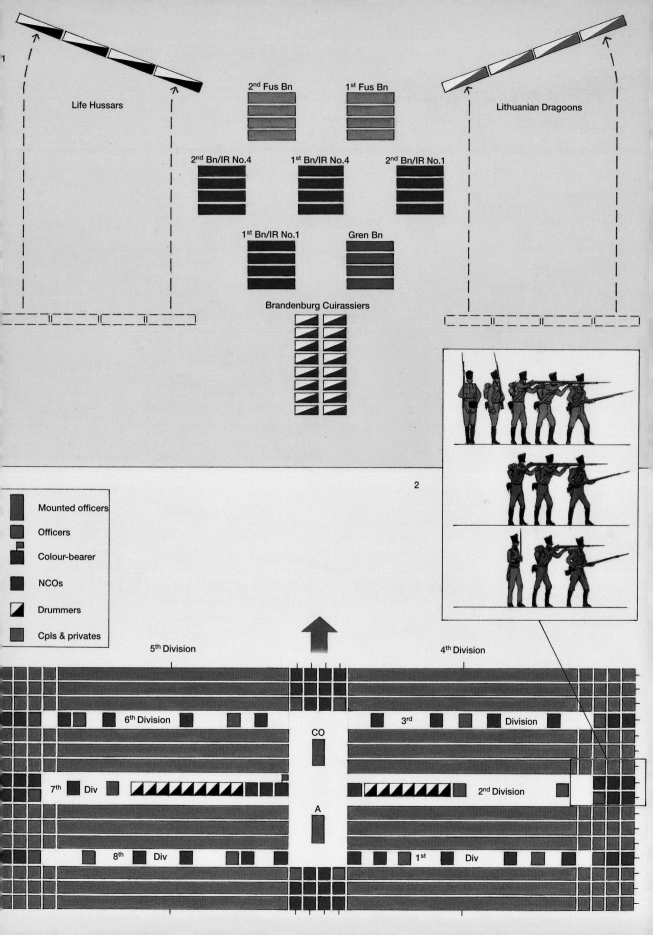

1

Life Hussars

2nd Fus Bn

1st Fus Bn

Lithuanian Dragoons

2nd Bn/IR No.4

1st Bn/IR No.4

2nd Bn/IR No.1

1st Bn/IR No.1

Gren Bn

Brandenburg Cuirassiers

2

Mounted officers

Officers

Colour-bearer

NCOs

Drummers

Cpls & privates

5th Division

4th Division

6th Division

3rd Division

CO

7th Div

2nd Division

A

8th Div

1st Div

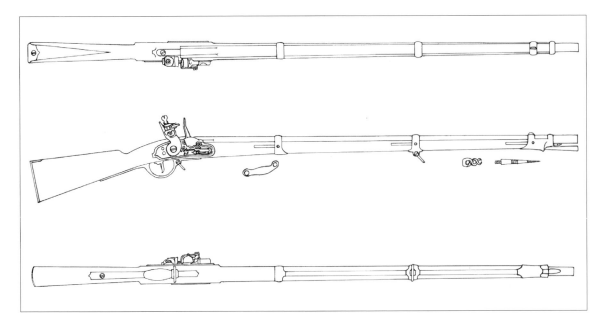

ABOVE AND OPPOSITE
The 'New Prussian' musket, 1809 pattern, was a modernized weapon with a shielded brass priming pan (for protection against weather, and corrosion), and brass barrel bands (for easier stripping). Tests in 1813 recorded 76 per cent hits on a target representing an enemy line at a range of 100 paces, similar to the French Charleville. This weapon was supposed to be issued to the whole of the infantry, but lack of funds meant that only a few were manufactured before the end of the Napoleonic Wars. In practice the Prussians used a miscellany of firearms in 1815, including several locally manufactured patterns, captured French weapons, and others supplied by friendly armies. The Prussian infantry were much worse equipped in 1815 than they had been in 1806. (By kind permission of Biblio-Verlag, Osnabrück)

battalions in the next line, and the senior musketeer and grenadier battalions in the last. The columns of infantry would then close up in 'squares' (see our Plate G2). Two regiments of cavalry would then sweep around the squares to meet the enemy cavalry, while the third regiment remained in reserve.

The demands of war in 1813–15 led to changes in the use of brigades, although the principles of mutual support were generally maintained.

1813–14

On the outbreak of war against France in spring 1813 the remainder of the army that had not gone to Russia (see commentary, Plate D) was mobilized, along with battalions of reservists or *Krümper*. These latter were amalgamated into the field brigades, which now varied in strength from six to ten battalions. A militia, the *Landwehr*, was also raised, but did not see action on a large scale until the campaign of autumn 1813. Militia battalions were attached to each field brigade, sometimes inflating its size to such an extent that it had to be divided into two. The mass mobilization of unevenly trained manpower greatly increased the size of the army, but diluted its quality. (The expanded brigades, although now in effect divisions, were still referred to as brigades, as – confusingly – were the two formations into which some had been divided.)

The Prussian army suffered heavy losses in autumn 1813, and when Blücher's Army of Silesia entered France early in 1814 it had been reorganized into a vanguard, a reserve of the vanguard, three field brigades, reserve cavalry and artillery. The light troops were concentrated in the vanguard, the line troops in the field brigades. When war broke out again unexpectedly in spring 1815 the army was in the throes of a major reorganization, due in part to changes in the territories ruled by the Prussian monarchy.

THE CAVALRY

The 1812 Cavalry Regulations were based on a provisional Instruction published in 1810. These regulations were not regarded as progressive;

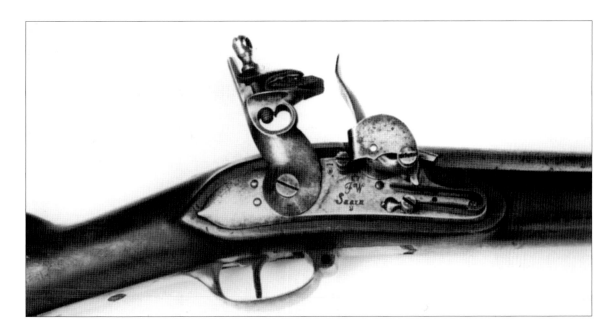

movements were slower than previously, and the role of the cavalry was subordinated to that of the infantry. A number of formations given in the regulations, such as an attack column similar to that used by the infantry, were considered impracticable for battlefield use.

As mentioned, the cavalry was normally deployed behind the infantry, where it was to await the attacks of enemy cavalry. It would move to meet these in the flank once the enemy cavalry had taken casualties from the fire of the Prussian infantry and artillery. Attacks were to be made in line, in echelons, or in columns by squadron, and the corners of infantry squares were to be targeted. Normally only the last 80 paces of an attack were to be made at the charge, with the previous 220 paces being made at the gallop. Practice attacks made on the parade ground covered 600 to 800 paces, with the fourth troop of the squadron being left behind in expectation of conducting a pursuit, as was previous practice. The use of larger bodies of cavalry than those attached to an infantry brigade was not mentioned in the regulations, partly due to the fact that when they were published in 1812 the largest formation in the restricted Prussian army was the brigade. The massive expansion of the army in 1813, using only partially trained manpower, demanded improvisation. Much of the cavalry attached to the infantry brigades was then transferred to the reserve of the newly formed army corps, where it needed time to adjust to the new circumstances.

While the regulations betray a degree of timidity in the use of cavalry, in practice the Prussian cavalry was often bold when in action, and it played a significant role in battles like Haynau on 26 May 1813, Liebertwolkwitz on 14 October 1813, and Ligny on 16 June 1815.

Liebertwolkwitz – the opening phase of the battle of Leipzig – was the largest and most decisive cavalry action of the era, and it saw the Allied cavalry (particularly the Prussians) gaining the upper hand over French cavalry commanded by no less a figure than Marshal Murat. The French cavalry had been decimated in Russia the previous year, and although veterans from the Peninsula had been brought in to strengthen the army in Germany they did not prove to be as adept as their opponents. The cavalry action commenced at 11 a.m., with two Russian hussar regiments halting an attack by two French

When deploying skirmishers from an attack column of line infantry, the third-rank men would form up in skirmish divisions on each flank, before moving forwards to deploy into a skirmish line, with the usual supports to their rear. (Hartwig, *Elementar-Taktik*; author's collection)

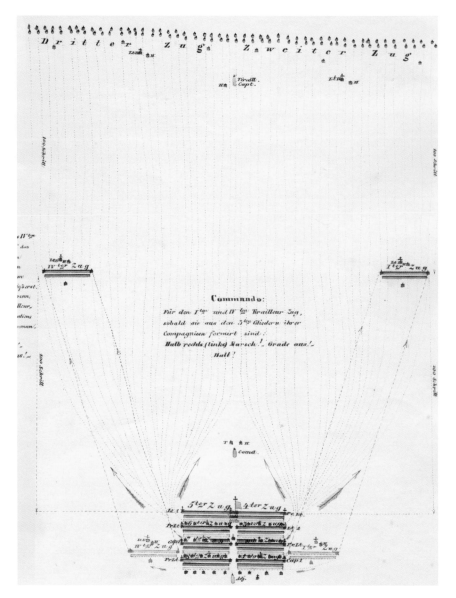

cavalry divisions. Murat's cavalry staged two further attacks that afternoon, but on both occasions the Prussians gained their flanks and drove back the French (see Plate E1). Thus the regimental history of the Brandenburg Cuirassier Regiment:

> The leading regiment, the East Prussian Cuirassiers, advanced at a trot in line, with the Silesian Cuirassier Regiment at a short distance to its left. Behind them came the Neumark Dragoon Regiment. At that moment, the Brandenburg Cuirassier Regiment received an order from General von Roeder [commander of the Prussian Reserve Cavalry] to follow the East Prussians at a walk so that should things go wrong, they could halt and protect the cavalry to their front. Just then, the East Prussian Cuirassier Regiment approached the place of combat, while the [Russian] Sumy hussars moved up to protect the Russian battery

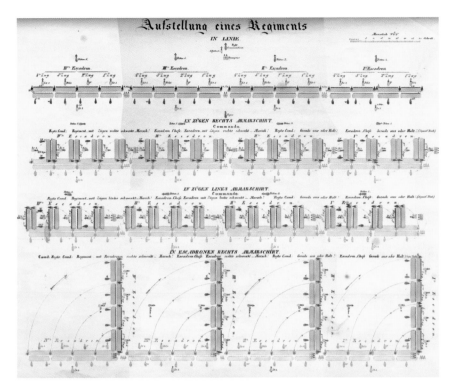

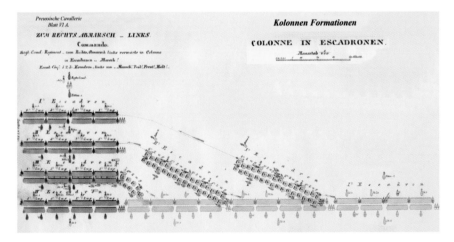

LEFT

Formation of a cavalry regiment. The top line of the diagram shows a regiment of four squadrons drawn up in line; the second and third lines show how a regiment would move to the left or right by troops; and the bottom line, the regiment moving to the right by squadrons.
(Hartwig, *Elementar-Taktik*; author's collection)

LEFT AND BOTTOM

These diagrams show two different methods for a cavalry regiment deployed in line to form a column of squadrons – (above) to the left, and (below) to the right. Either method could be used in either direction.
(Hartwig, *Elementar-Taktik*; author's collection)

General Yorck doffing his cap
to men of the Life Regiment
as they pass him in column
of march after the battle of
Wartenburg, 3 October 1813.
(Carl Röchling; author's
collection)

and charged the enemy. Artillery fire enfiladed its left flank, while strong
enemy forces arrived in front of it, so it was forced to withdraw. Count
Pahlen [commander of the Vanguard] immediately directed the East
Prussian Cuirassiers to the right, past the right flank of the Sumy hussars
diagonally against the enemy's left flank. In the same direction, but
further to the right of this regiment, he sent two squadrons of the Silesian
Uhlan Regiment to follow up behind the East Prussian Cuirassiers.

The East Prussian Cuirassier Regiment now staged a brilliant
charge against the enemy, forcing them to fall back a long distance.
However, as the enemy brought up significant forces and deployed
substantial reserves amounting to around three times our strength and
that of the Sumy hussars, we had to fall back. This almost invariably led
to a large part of this combined mass of cavalry, under close pursuit,
mixed together, riding towards the front line of our regiment. Major
von Loebell [provisional commander of the Brandenburg Cuirassiers]
had the regiment halt immediately, so extending the intervals between
the squadrons, letting one of the neighbouring troops move away.
The gaps so created allowed most of the retreating mass of cavalry to
pass through or go round our flanks and so force the pursuing enemy
to break off, although on our left the enemy continued their pursuit as
we had not deployed a reserve there.

Now that our front line was clear, we could see a line of French
dragoons in good order standing about 60 paces in front of us, who
started firing odd shots at us with their carbines. About 600 paces to

their rear, a second line of enemy cavalry was moving up at a trot. To our left, about 50 paces behind our left flank a grass-covered ditch about 4 feet wide ran diagonally at an angle to our front line. This may have been the reason why part of the French cavalry that would otherwise have outflanked us on the left, but was not able to cross the ditch, instead built up into a column about ten to 12 troops strong. This, like the remainder of their line, halted a good 20 paces in front of us and about as much to our left.

This was the moment when, on the orders of Lt von Gillern commanding the 3rd Troop of our 4th Squadron, the two flank troops wheeled left and charged the enemy columns of troops. The two other troops, under Rittmeister [cavalry captain] von Zieten, followed them. The enemy column turned around and was pushed towards the ditch, causing a larger number of enemy dragoons to fall into it, where they were killed or taken prisoner by Cossacks that had rushed over. While this combat involving the 4th Squadron was going on, the other three squadrons doubled towards the line of enemy cavalry standing in front of them, forcing it back towards the supporting enemy cavalry, which also turned around. Noticing that the enemy on the far side of the ditch… that [had been] pursuing the mass of cavalry in the rear of our position was [now] advancing with not insignificant forces, and that if they were to turn around they could easily take our flank and rear, he decided against a further pursuit and had the call to rally sounded.

The regiment withdrew without being pursued to about 200 paces to the rear of where it started its advance, [and] the East Prussian Cuirassier Regiment moved next to it, but this time on its right. The enemy too had rallied, and attacked us again. We then undertook a second attack along with the East Prussian Cuirassier Regiment, which resulted in the enemy being chased away again, this time as far as Wachau. The artillery fire from there compelled us to withdraw. The regiment again rallied, gaining ground this time; there was a moment of quiet when, at least on this flank, the fighting died down.

An analysis of the tactical employment of the Prussian cavalry at Liebertwolkwitz shows the use of the line, and advances in echelon by entire regiments, with individual squadrons and even troops being used at the right moment to gain the enemy's flank and achieve local successes. Formed units were held in reserve to cover the advance, and to protect beaten units that were withdrawing; they then covered these units while they rallied, and engaged in further attacks. The ebb and flow of the battle was reflected in the tactical use of cavalry units, and the victor was normally the side that had the last formed reserve to commit to combat.

THE ARTILLERY

The 1812 Artillery Regulations also concentrated largely on how the guns were to be used in support of an infantry brigade, and there was no provision for the use of massed batteries in classic Napoleonic style. This was not an oversight, but simply a reflection of the reality – the shrunken Prussian army in 1812 could only operate as part of a larger alliance, and was not permitted an artillery reserve. On mobilization in spring 1813, and the rapid expansion

(continued on page 60)

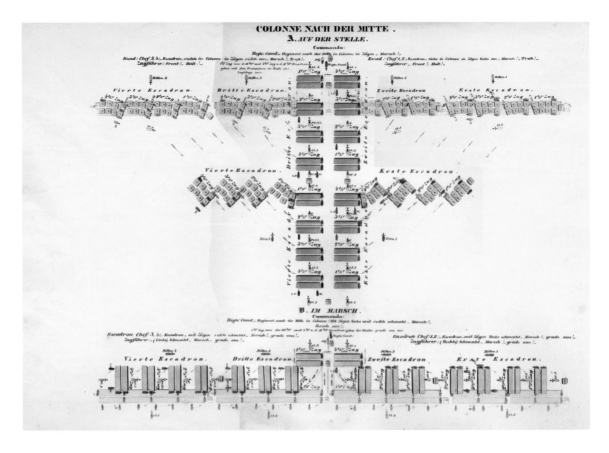

Ways for a cavalry regiment deployed in line to form a 'column by the centre' – i.e. of paired troops. (Hartwig, *Elementar-Taktik*; author's collection)

H TWO PRUSSIAN BRIGADES ATTACK TOWARDS PLANCENOIT, 18 JUNE 1815

At about 4.30pm on the day of Waterloo, as the French cavalry attacks on Wellington's centre and right at Mont St Jean were building towards their height, the 15th Bde (Losthin, c. 6,100 infantry) and 16th Bde (Hiller, c. 6,200) of Bülow's Prussian IV Corps prepared for their first attack of the day. They could hear the noise of battle to their west, but due to the tall crops and patches of woodland they could see little ahead other than the spire of Plancenoit church about a mile to their left front. Probably all that the advancing Prussian infantry could see of the French were the heads of the foremost cavalry troopers, and infantry skirmishers from each side would bump into each other as they moved through the crops. Facing the Prussians on higher ground were two French infantry divisions from Lobau's VI Corps: the 19th (Simmer – 9 battalions, 4,000 men) and the 20th (Jeanin – 6 battalions, 3,000 men). These were supported by three divisions of cavalry: the 1st (Jacquinot – 4 regiments, 1,600 men), 5th (Subervie – 3 regiments, 1,200 men), and 3rd (Domon – 3 regiments, 900 men). The Prussian deployment shows how the theory of the 1812 Regulations was adapted when faced with the practical realities of terrain, and with the change in the composition of brigades due to wartime expansion.

A screen of cavalry squadrons was thrown forwards (in front of Losthin, the 600 men of the 6th Hussars, while the 450 troopers of the 2nd Neumark Landwehr Cavalry covered Hiller); from their saddles, the troopers had a better line of sight above the tall corps. There was by now only one battalion of regular fusiliers in each brigade, with two battalions of regular musketeers and six of Landwehr. Losthin's Bde comprised the 18th Infantry and 3rd and 4th Silesian Landwehr, Hiller's the 15th Infantry and 1st and 2nd Silesian Landwehr. The fusilier battalions were thrown forwards to form skirmish lines. Bülow needed to link up with Wellington's threatened left flank; he sent two of Losthin's battalions (one of regulars, the other of Landwehr) swinging right towards the Chateau de Frichermont and the village of Smohain, and a similar pair of Hiller's units left towards Virère Wood. Meanwhile, each brigade formed its remaining one regular and five Landwehr battalions into two waves of attack columns, deploying from columns of march as they arrived on the field.

Inset: Colour party of regular musketeers in the attack. From 1813 only a single *Avancierfahne* was carried by each battalion. The colour party was officially formed of one officer and seven senior NCOs; the colour-bearer himself made use of his sidearm, and the others carried muskets or carbines with fixed bayonets.

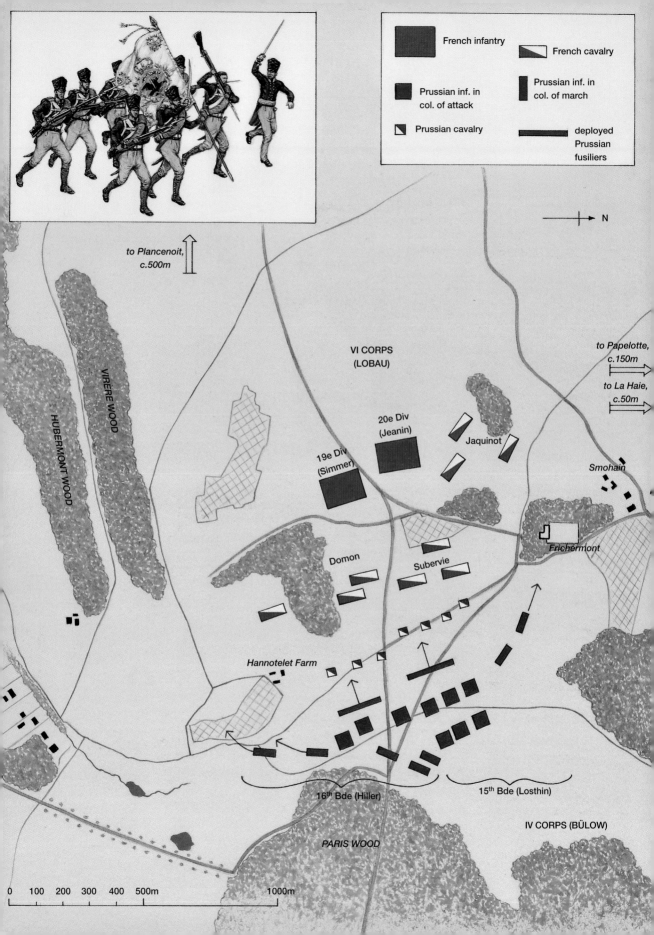

Legend

■ French infantry	◨ French cavalry
■ Prussian inf. in col. of attack	▮ Prussian inf. in col. of march
◪ Prussian cavalry	▬ deployed Prussian fusiliers

N →

to Plancenoit, c.500m ⬆

VI CORPS (LOBAU)

to Papelotte, c.150m →

to La Haie, c.50m →

VIRÈRE WOOD

HUBERMONT WOOD

20e Div (Jeanin)

Jaquinot

Smohain

19e Div (Simmer)

Frichermont

Domon

Subervie

Hannotelet Farm

16ᵗʰ Bde (Hiller)

15ᵗʰ Bde (Losthin)

PARIS WOOD

IV CORPS (BÜLOW)

0 100 200 300 400 500m   1000m

Spirited painting of men of the 1st Pomeranian Infantry Regiment driving back the Imperial Guard with a bayonet charge during the battle for Plancenoit on 18 June 1815. (Carl Röchling; author's collection)

of the army during that summer's armistice, this problem was addressed in an improvised fashion, with the Allied armies allocating artillery batteries to a general reserve, normally held at corps level.

Until 1806 the 12-pdr had been the main battle cannon, leading to problems of mobility, but now that the field artillery role was envisaged as limited to infantry support the more mobile 6-pdr was used instead. More mobility meant less effect, however, and penny-packets of 12-pdrs were often brought up from the reserve to crucial points on the battlefield. From the start of the Wars of Liberation in 1813 the lack of heavy battlefield artillery was apparent, but the circumstances prevented any resolution of this problem. The experience of war from 1813 led to all artillery officers being mounted wherever possible, with the crews riding on the draft horses, as did the horse artillery already.[3]

WATERLOO, 1815

After Napoleon's first abdication in 1814 the multinational Congress of Vienna set about redrawing the map of Europe; Prussia lost territory mainly in the east, and gained new territories mainly in the west. The old system of recruiting largely from the peasantry and exempting the more educated classes

3 For further details of the tactical handling of Prussian artillery in the Wars of Liberation, see MAA 381, *Prussian Staff & Specialist Troops 1791–1815*.

was modified; the number of exemptions was reduced, as was the reliance on a substantial number of full-time volunteers, in favour of this broader conscription. The old system of local canton recruitment was extended over larger areas, to provide manpower for permanent army corps containing a mixture of all arms.

However, this process was interrupted when Napoleon escaped from Elba and initiated what became known as the 'Hundred Days'. The Prussian army had to be mobilized while in the midst of a major reorganization. Four army corps were improvised to participate in the campaign in the Netherlands; these contained a mixture of troops from various parts of the kingdom, and also a number of foreign units that had yet to be properly integrated into the Prussian army. This Army of the Lower Rhine was probably the worst in terms of manpower and quality of equipment that Prussia fielded throughout the Napoleonic Wars.

Each of the four army corps consisted of four field brigades, reserve cavalry and reserve artillery. Generally, a field brigade consisted of nine battalions of infantry, with artillery support. On 8 June 1815, Marshal Blücher had Gen von Grolman of his staff issue an Instruction to the brigade commanders, which read, in part, as follows:

'The brigade formation is already laid down in the Regulations *[1812 Reglement]* and it has been confirmed in practice by the experience of the last war. As the brigades now consist of nine battalions, they will as a rule be deployed as follows [the light troops being to the fore]:

Two light battalions
xxxxxx   xxxxxx

Four battalions
xxxxxx   xxxxxx   xxxxxx   xxxxxx

One light battalion   Two battalions
xxxxxx   xxxxxx   xxxxxx

One 6-pdr battery
xxxxxxxx

Two squadrons
xxxx   xxxx

'The artillery and cavalry will be deployed according to circumstances and terrain, and have no set positions. As a rule, however, the cavalry should not be separated from the brigade. Only rarely may an exception be made – to pursue the enemy, or when all the cavalry is detached from the corps.

'Whenever an army corps requires a vanguard, an entire brigade will be designated for this purpose and will receive the necessary cavalry from the reserve cavalry (as a rule two regiments, since the cavalry regiments are weak) and one horse battery. If circumstances require, half a battery of 12-pdrs can be added.

'In open terrain, the reserve cavalry must immediately follow the vanguard in support. In other circumstances, the corps commanding general is responsible for its disposition.

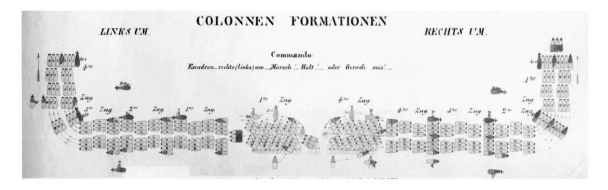

This diagram shows how a cavalry squadron in line – see our Plate E2 for formation – formed into a column, either to the left or to the right. (Hartwig, *Elementar-Taktik*; author's collection)

'Those Landwehr regiments that have yet to designate one battalion as the light battalion are to immediately select the one judged by its commander as the best suited for this purpose. This battalion, as well as the third rank of all battalions, must be well trained in skirmishing and individual combat.'

As mentioned, the peacetime brigades of 1808–12 had been enlarged with reserve and militia units during the campaigns of 1813. It was customary to divide the responsibilities of command of such large formations among several senior officers. For example, in 1815, while MajGen von Pirch II was in overall command of the 2nd Brigade, LtCol von Stach commanded its infantry. The brigade commander controlled three subordinate commanders, of the infantry, the cavalry and the artillery, and from his brigade headquarters could thus co-ordinate and direct his units in battle far more effectively than his predecessor in command of a temporary tactical brigade in 1806.

Despite its many handicaps, the Army of the Lower Rhine – commanded by a soldier who had served under Frederick the Great – proved in the end equal to its task.

SELECT BIBLIOGRAPHY

Anonymous:
1806 – Das Preussische Offizierkorps und die Untersuching der Kiregsereignisse (Berlin, 1906)
Exerzir-Reglement fuer die Artillerie der Koeniglich Preussischen Armee (Berlin, 1812)
Exerzir-Reglement fuer die Infanterie der Koeniglich Preussischen Armee (Berlin, 1812)
Das Preussische Heer der Befreiungskriege, 3 vols (German General Staff, Berlin, 1912–14/20, r/p 1982)
Rangliste der Koeniglichen Preussischen Armee fuer das Jahr 1806 (r/p Osnabrück, 1976)
Reglement fuer die Koeniglich Preussische Infanterie (Bielefeld, 1788)
Stammliste aller Regimenter und Corps der Koeniglich-Preussischen Armee fuer das Jahr 1806 (r/p Osnabrück, 1975)

Bressonnet, Pascal, *Études Tactiques sur la Campagne de 1806* (Paris, 1909)
Delbrück, Hans, *Das Leben des Feldmarcshalls Grafen Neidhardt von Gneisenau* – 2 vols (4th edn, Berlin, 1920)
Droysen, Johann Gustav, *Das Leben des Feldmarschalls Grafen Yorck von Wartenburg* (various edns)

Fiedler, Siegried, *Grundriss der Militaer- und Kriegsgeschichte* – Vol 2; *Das Zeitalter der Franzoesixhen Revolution und Napoleons* – Vol 3; *Napoleon gegen Preussen* (Munich, 1976 & 1978)

Friedrich, Rudolf von, *Geschichte des Herbstfeldzuges 1813* – Vol 2 (Berlin, 1904)

Goltz, Colmar Freiherr von der, *Rossbach und Jena* (Berlin, 1883)

Henderson, Ernest F., *Bluecher and the Uprising of Prussia against Napoleon 1806–1815* (London & New York, 1911)

Jany, Curt, *Der Preussische Kavalleriedienst vor 1806* (Berlin, 1906)

Jany, Curt, *Die Gefechtsausbildung der Preussischen Infanterie von 1806* (r/p Wiesbaden, 1982)

Jany, Curt, *Geschichte der Preussischen Armee vom 15. Jahrhundert bis 1914* (Vol 3) *1763–1807*; (Vol 4) *Das Koeniglich Preussische Armee und das Deitsche Reichsheer 1807 bis 1914* (r/p Osnabrück, 1967)

Kling, Constantin, *Die Kirassier- und Dragoner-Regimenter seit Angang des 18. Jahrhunderts bis zur Reorganisation der Armee 1808* (Weimar, 1906)

Krippenstapel, Friedrich & Richard Knoetel, *Die Preussichen Husaren von der aeltesten Zeiten bis zur Gegenwart* (Berlin, 1883)

Lehmann, Max, *Scharnhorst*, 2 vols (Leipzig, 1886–87)

Lehner, Dieter, *Die altpreussischen Schutzwafen un ihre Beiwaffen 1713–1823* (Krefeld, 1973)

Malinowsky, Louis von & Robert von Bonin, *Geschichte der brandenburgisch-preussischen Artillerie*, 3 vols (Berlin, 1840–42)

Pelet-Narbonne, G. von, *Geschichte der Brandenburg-Preussischen Reiterei von der Zeiten des Grossen Kurfuersten bis zur Gegenwart* (Vol 1); *Die Alte Armee vom Grossen Kurfuersten dis zum Frieden von Tilsit* (Berlin, 1905)

Unger, W. von, *Bluecher*, 2 vols (Berlin, 1907–08)

Wirtgen, A., *Die Preussischen Handfeuerwaffen 1700–1806* (Osnabrück, 1976) – this is Vol 8 of Part IV of Hans Blackwenn (ed), *Das Altpreussiche Heer – Erscheinungsbild und Wesen 1713–1807*

Despite the emphasis on close-order drills and the regulation of the use of skirmishers, much of the fighting in the battles of 1813–15 took place in the streets of towns and villages. Order soon broke down, and combat was undertaken by *ad hoc* battle-groups, making frequent use of the bayonet and the musket butt in hand-to-hand fighting. This confusion is conveyed in Northen's painting of street fighting in Plancenoit on the evening of 18 June 1815. (Author's collection)

INDEX

Page numbers in **bold** refer to illustrations